BrightRED Study Guide

Curriculum for Excellence

N4

ADMINISTRATION and IT

Jane Sturrock

First published in 2015 by:
Bright Red Publishing Ltd
1 Torphichen Street
Edinburgh
EH3 8HX

Copyright © Bright Red Publishing Ltd 2015

Cover image © Caleb Rutherford

All rights reserved. No part of this publication may be reproduced, stored in a retrieval system, or transmitted in any form or by any means, electronic, mechanical, photocopying, recording or otherwise, without prior permission in writing from the publisher.

The rights of Jane Sturrock to be identified as the author of this work have been asserted by her in accordance with sections 77 and 78 of the Copyright, Designs and Patents Act 1988.

A CIP record for this book is available from the British Library

ISBN 978-1-906736-45-3

With thanks to:
PDQ Digital Media Solutions Ltd (layout), Clodagh Burke (edit)

Cover design by Caleb Rutherford – e i d e t i c

Acknowledgements
Every effort has been made to seek all copyright holders. If any have been overlooked, then Bright Red Publishing will be delighted to make the necessary arrangements.

Permission has been sought from all relevant copyright holders and Bright Red Publishing are grateful for the use of the following:
National 4 Administration and IT Course Specification © Scottish Qualifications Authority (p 4); shironosov/iStockphoto (p 6); i_frontier/iStockphoto (p 7); stockyimages/iStockphoto (p 8); Minerva Studio/iStockphoto (p 9); innovatedcaptures/iStockphoto (p 10); ginosphotos/iStockphoto (p 12); Richard Duszczak/Cartoon Motivators (p 13); kilukilu/iStockphoto (p 14); Naypong/Shutterstock (p 14); Caleb Rutherford (p 15); koya79/iStockphoto (p 16); racorn/Shutterstock (p 17); andresrimaging/iStockphoto (p 18); ChameleonsEye /Shutterstock (p 19); Sean_Warren/iStockphoto (p 20); Michael & Christa Richert/freeimages.com (pp 22, 24, 26); Caleb Rutherford (p 72); fotek/iStockphoto (p 73); Caleb Rutherford (p 74).

Printed and bound in the UK by Charlesworth Press

CONTENTS

INTRODUCING NATIONAL 4 ADMINISTRATION

The aim of this book is to provide practical help and tips for students and teachers alike with regards to the knowledge and understanding and ICT skills required for the SQA National 4 Administration and IT course as outlined below in the course specification. However, many of the IT skills covered in this book would be relevant to anyone wishing to improve their competency in this area.

THE NATIONAL 4 COURSE

The N4 Administration and IT Course comprises three mandatory Units and an Added Value Unit. While this book has been broadly divided into the three mandatory units, it must be remembered that many of the skills and the knowledge and understanding permeate all the units and they cannot be completed in isolation. The practice assignments at the end of each unit reflect this and **all** tasks have relevance to the Added Value Unit.

National 4 Administration and IT Course Specification (C701 74)

Mandatory skills, knowledge and understanding	Administrative Practices	IT Solutions for Administrators	Communication in Administration
Skills, qualities and attributes required of administrators	✔		
Basic skills in using the following IT applications: word processing, spreadsheets, databases, presentations and desktop publishing, in familiar administrative contexts		✔	✔
Skills in organising and supporting small-scale events	✔	✔	✔
Basic skills in using technology, including the internet, for electronic communication and investigation in familiar administrative contexts			✔
Basic skills in organising, processing and communicating simple information in familiar administrative contexts		✔	✔
Knowledge and understanding of key legislation affecting employees in the workplace	✔		
Knowledge and understanding of the key features of good customer care	✔		

Further mandatory information with regards to the Course Specification, Unit Specifications and the Added Value Unit Specification can be found on the SQA website: http://www.sqa.org.uk/sqa/47431.html

Each of the mandatory units has a number of outcomes. To gain a pass at National 4 level, you must pass all outcomes within each of the three mandatory units as well as the Added Value Unit. **All** of these are marked by your classroom teacher.

The specific outcomes and standards that you must achieve for each unit are as follows:

Administrative practices

Outcome 1

Provide an overview of administration in the workplace by:

1 Naming the main tasks, skills and qualities of an administrative assistant

2 Outlining the key features of good customer care

3 Outlining the key employee responsibilities in terms of health and safety

4 Outlining the key employee responsibilities in terms of the security of people, property and information

Outcome 2

Carry out administrative tasks in the context of organising and supporting small-scale events, according to a simple brief, by:

1 Carrying out straightforward planning tasks for the event

2 Editing documents to support the event

3 Carrying out follow-up activities

IT solutions for administrators

Outcome 1

Use functions of a spreadsheet in line with a given task by:

1 Editing a spreadsheet, applying simple formulae

2 Sorting data within the worksheet

3 Creating a simple chart from a specified range

Outcome 2

Use functions of a flat database in line with a given task by:

1 Populating a database, using forms

2 Editing a database

3 Manipulating information by searching and sorting

4 Creating a simple report

Outcome 3

Use functions of word processing in line with a given task by:

1 Creating and editing simple business documents, complying with the prescribed house style

2 Creating a simple table and sorting the data

3 Importing data into a simple business document

Communication in administration

Outcome 1

Use technology to gather information in line with a simple brief by:

1 Searching for and extracting simple information from the internet

2 Searching for and extracting simple information using an internal network (intranet)

Outcome 2

Use functions of technology to prepare and communicate simple information in line with a simple brief:

1 Using multimedia to create a simple presentation

2 Using desktop publishing to produce a simple document

3 Using an electronic method to communicate information

HOW TO USE THIS BOOK

Instructions and information, including screen dumps where relevant, have been provided in a logical and progressive way in order to help you to develop and build upon your skills as you work through the exercises and when direct support from your teacher is not available.

Every attempt has been made to ensure all the skills and knowledge and understanding elements specified in each of the Unit Specifications have been included either within this book or included in the exercises available on the digital zone (www.brightredbooks.net). In some instances, extension tasks have also been included for those students progressing to National 5 Administration and IT or entering further study, employment or training.

Your feedback on this book would be most welcome!

TASKS, SKILLS AND QUALITIES OF AN ADMINISTRATOR

ADMINISTRATORS

WHAT DOES AN ADMINISTRATIVE ASSISTANT DO?

The role of Administrative Assistant exists in many different organisations – banks, schools, hospitals, doctors' and dentists' surgeries – and even small businesses like local hairdressers and restaurants will have someone who is employed to carry out administrative tasks. If the business is very small then the owners may 'do the paperwork' themselves!

As a general rule, an Administrative Assistant is responsible for the day-to-day office tasks that ensure the business runs smoothly and that others can do their jobs. An Administrative Assistant provides help and support within the organisation and carries out a wide range of tasks which include:

- making diary appointments and arranging meetings
- answering the telephone and taking messages
- dealing with the mail – mail received by the company has to be sorted, opened, date stamped and distributed to the relevant people and letters and parcels being sent out should be properly addressed with the correct postage and taken to the Post Office to meet collection deadlines
- photocopying documents and making up booklets
- filing documents in the correct place so that they can be found again quickly when required
- keeping databases up-to-date, for example, changing an employee's records when they move to a new address, and recording financial and other information using spreadsheets
- making sure there is enough stationery and office supplies
- reception duties including greeting and welcoming visitors
- word processing documents such as letters, memos and reports
- arranging travel and accommodation for staff going on business trips

DON'T FORGET

The duties, tasks and responsibilities involved in a job are detailed in a document called a *job description*.

WHAT SKILLS AND QUALITIES SHOULD AN ADMINISTRATIVE ASSISTANT HAVE?

As well as having formal qualifications to be able to do a job there is also the requirement to have particular skills and qualities.

A **skill** is having the ability to do something well. Some people have a natural talent for doing certain things like singing or drawing but it is possible to learn new skills and improve upon existing skills, for example, IT skills.

The skills that an administrative assistant should have include:

- Effective communication skills – this includes verbal, listening and writing skills. Communication is a two-way process which means you must be able to listen carefully to what is being said, seek clarification and ask questions if unsure and pass on information accurately and without error.

- Computer literacy and IT skills – being able to use a variety of computer programs including word processing, spreadsheet, database and presentation software as well as being able to use the internet and e-mail.

- Problem-solving skills – being able to anticipate problems before they occur and come up with solutions when they do.
- Organisational skills – being able to work in a methodical manner and know where everything is. For example, you should be able to quickly find a specific document without wasting any time. Being able to multi-task is a must!
- Time management skills – being able to schedule and plan ahead and prioritise tasks, ensuring those that have a high priority are completed first (some tasks can wait to be completed later). However, all deadlines must be met!
- Teamwork and interpersonal skills – being able to get on well with others and work as a responsible member of a team. This includes working with minimum supervision and using your initiative, but knowing when to ask for help and advice.

WHAT QUALITIES SHOULD AN ADMINISTRATIVE ASSISTANT HAVE?

A **quality** is a personal attribute – something which describes the type of person you are, for example, patient, friendly and having a good sense of humour.

The qualities that an Administrative Assistant should have include being:

- Hard working and conscientious – taking the job seriously, completing tasks and taking pride in doing everything well.
- Accurate and careful – understanding the need to produce error-free work and taking the time to check everything very carefully. Paying attention to detail is very important.
- Reliable, punctual and dependable – turning up for work on time every day and completing tasks without supervision.
- Enthusiastic – taking an interest in and enjoying the job.
- Honest and trustworthy – can be trusted to handle anything of value including money and confidential information.
- Flexible and willing to learn – being able to cope with change and keen to learn new skills and attend training courses.
- Polite, friendly and helpful – understanding the importance of being courteous and giving assistance to colleagues, visitors and customers.

When a vacancy arises in an organisation both a *job description* and a *person specification* are drawn up. Using both of these documents, a job advertisement can be created and put up on noticeboards, circulated to job centres or published in newspapers or online. Anyone interested in applying for the job will either send in their CV or complete an application form. The organisation will review all applications and decide which candidates they would like to interview. An interview gives the opportunity for the organisation to find out more about the candidate, and for the candidate to learn more about the job and the company. The organisation then selects the person they want to do the job and sends out a letter of appointment. All unsuccessful applicants, both those who have been interviewed and those who have not, should be written to. An Administrative assistant would provide help and support at every stage of this process.

DON'T FORGET

The skills and qualities of the ideal person to do a job are listed in a document called a *person specification*.

DON'T FORGET

A CV (curriculum vitae) is a summary of someone's life – their personal details, qualifications, work history and experience and interests and hobbies.

THINGS TO DO AND THINK ABOUT

Draft up your CV – in addition to personal details include any qualifications you already have as well as those subjects you are currently sitting. Also include a brief paragraph about your skills and qualities and give details of any extracurricular activities you are involved in and your hobbies and interests. A well-written CV is your chance to sell yourself to a potential employer!

CUSTOMER CARE

CUSTOMER SERVICE

KEY FEATURES OF GOOD CUSTOMER SERVICE

Focusing on customer service is the key to success in business. Customers not only consider which product to buy but they are also looking for suppliers who can deliver quickly, offer support when things go wrong and have well-informed staff who can offer advice.

In order to keep customers satisfied and provide good customer service in a fair and consistent way, organisations will have a **customer service policy** and will put a **customer service procedure** in place so that all staff will know exactly how to deal with customers.

The characteristics of good customer service are:

- Good communication – employees should respond to customers' letters and e-mails quickly and should answer the phone promptly and politely within an agreed number of rings. Customers may get fed up waiting and go elsewhere – no-one likes to feel invisible and be ignored!
- Only making promises that can be kept – reliability is one of the keys to having good customer relations. Customers will become frustrated and angry if their expectations are not met, for example, if a customer has been promised a delivery at a particular time on a particular day and it doesn't happen, they will become very annoyed.
- Going the extra mile – if customers get more than they expect they will remember this in the future. Staff should take the extra step and add extra value to the customer's experience. For example, if the item the customer is looking for is not in stock, staff should offer to find out if another branch has it and whether it can be posted out to them.
- Providing staff with training in customer care – staff should always be helpful and courteous and knowledgeable about the products they are selling. All employees should have a copy of the customer care policy.
- Offering customers the opportunity to provide feedback on their experience – the organisation should survey their customers regularly, for example, by conducting phone surveys, online surveys or by post to make sure that customers are satisfied and to find out if there are any areas of weakness that can be improved upon. Customers will appreciate being asked their opinions.
- Dealing with customer complaints and rectifying any problems promptly – employees should follow an agreed procedure for dealing with complaints and ensure all complaints are given attention and none are ignored. Organisations should use complaints as a learning experience in order to avoid repeating the same mistakes.
- Providing good after-sales service – this will encourage the customer to buy the product, for example, if you buy a bike you might get free bike maintenance for a number of weeks.

DON'T FORGET

A **customer service policy** is a statement detailing the principles the organisation will adopt when conducting business and dealing with customers and the standards customers can expect. Policies don't need to be long or complicated – a couple of sentences may be all that is needed for each policy area.

DON'T FORGET

A **customer service procedure** describes the way the policy will be put into practice – who will do what, the order in which it will be done and what documentation is required.

THE BENEFITS OF GOOD CUSTOMER SERVICE

Providing good customer service will be beneficial to the organisation in a number of ways including:

- Satisfied customers will be loyal customers – customers will come back and buy again. It costs at least five times as much to gain a new customer than it does to keep an existing one.
- Happy customers will recommend the organisation to others – word-of-mouth recommendations bring in new customers for free, helping the business to grow.
- Recommendations from existing customers will improve the image of the organisation and give it a good reputation – customers will choose that organisation rather than a competitor.
- More customers will mean more sales and therefore increase the organisation's profits. The company will also have a bigger share of the market.
- Happy customers will mean happy employees – there will be fewer complaints to deal with and staff will be motivated and take pride in providing good customer service.
- Happy staff will stay with the organisation – there will be no need to spend time and money recruiting new employees and costs will be reduced.

IMPACT OF POOR CUSTOMER CARE

Poor customer service can negatively impact on a business in a number of ways, especially if the business is small and it relies on repeat business and positive word-of-mouth advertising for its success.

Poor customer service will mean:

- Loss of current customers – if customers are unhappy about the service they received they will be dissatisfied and they will not come back.
- Loss of future customers – customers who experience poor service will tell friends and family and people will have a negative opinion of the business before even setting foot in the door.
- Loss of reputation – the organisation will get a poor reputation through bad publicity if customers and staff talk about their bad experience. Other organisations may not want to do business with the company and potential employees might assume that if customers are treated poorly, so are staff.
- Loss of employees – employees who have to deal with unhappy customers may become stressed and will leave the organisation. It is costly and time-consuming to constantly have to recruit and train new staff. Customers might start to question the organisation's ability to manage and retain employees.
- Loss of profits – unhappy customers will look for another supplier and so the business will lose custom. Loss of customers means loss of sales and lower profits. There is a downward spiral with the organisation when trying to save money by reducing the number of staff and reducing customer service training and service levels spiral downwards even further. The business will eventually fail altogether.

THINGS TO DO AND THINK ABOUT

Can you think of situations where you have experienced both good customer service and poor customer service? What happened and how did that make you feel? Did your experience affect how you felt about the organisation? Would you go back there again?

HEALTH AND SAFETY AND THE SECURITY OF PEOPLE, PROPERTY AND INFORMATION

EMPLOYEES' RESPONSIBILITIES IN TERMS OF HEALTH AND SAFETY ISSUES

This includes the identification of hazards in the office and measures to ensure safe practice and completion of an accident report form.

Employers have legal responsibilities to ensure a safe and healthy workplace. They must carry out a risk assessment and decide what could cause harm and the precautions that could be taken to prevent any accidents. However, there are responsibilities that **employees** must take for their own wellbeing and that of their colleagues.

CURRENT LEGISLATION

Under current legislation an employee's duties are to:

- Take reasonable care of their own health and safety.
- Take reasonable care not to put other people – fellow employees and members of the public – at risk by what they do or don't do in the course of their work.
- Cooperate with their employer on health and safety matters.
- Not interfere with or misuse any equipment that has been provided for their health, safety or welfare including any personal protective equipment, for example, fire extinguishers, safety goggles or safety helmets.
- Follow instructions from the employer on health and safety matters and attend relevant health and safety training.
- Report hazards and defects observed in the workplace.

WHAT KINDS OF HEALTH PROBLEMS AND HAZARDS MIGHT YOU ENCOUNTER IN THE OFFICE?

Hazard	Actions that can be taken to prevent accidents
Slips and trips	- Work areas should be kept clear of obstructions - Any spillages should be cleaned up immediately and a danger sign should be used - All areas should be well lit, especially stairs - Any hazards such as torn carpets, trailing cables or faulty lighting should be reported immediately
Electrical equipment – electric shocks or burns from using faulty electrical equipment	- Electrical equipment should be tested for electrical safety at regular intervals and labelled with the date of the test - Electrical cables and plugs should be visually inspected at regular intervals by the user for damage - Any defective equipment should be reported immediately, then suitably labelled and taken out of use until the repair has been carried out. Repairs should only be carried out by suitably qualified engineers. - Electrical equipment should always be operated in accordance with manufacturers' instructions and training should be given - Liquids should be kept away from electrical equipment, for example, never drink beside computers - Sockets should never be overloaded

DON'T FORGET

A hazard is an item or a situation that may cause, or has the potential to cause, an accident.

DON'T FORGET

A risk is the likelihood of the hazard's potential being realised or the risk of the hazard actually happening.

DON'T FORGET

An accident is a separate, identifiable, unintended incident, which causes physical injury. Examples of injury include bone fractures, damage to eyesight and serious burns and scalding.

Display screen equipment (including desktop computers, laptops, touch-screens) – postural problems such as backache and neck pain, eyestrain, headaches, repetitive strain injury (RSI)	<ul><li>Where display screen equipment (DSE) is used, a workstation risk assessment must be carried out</li><li>Work should be planned to include regular breaks away from the computer, for example, take time out to do some filing</li><li>Users of display screen equipment have the right to a free eye test and be provided with special spectacles if needed</li><li>An anti-glare screen and controls should be used to adjust screen brightness</li><li>Visual display units (VDU) should be positioned away from direct light</li><li>Blinds should be closed</li><li>Wrist rests and adjustable keyboards should be used</li><li>Adjustable chairs with castors should be used</li><li>Employees should be given training and information on how to use equipment</li></ul>
Manual handling of heavy/bulky objects – back injuries	<ul><li>A risk assessment must be completed for lifting heavy and bulky loads that present a risk of injury</li><li>A trolley should be used to transport boxes of paper or other heavy items</li><li>High shelves should be used for light items only</li><li>Training in lifting techniques should be provided for anyone who undertakes the lifting of heavy loads</li></ul>
Fire	<ul><li>The storage of empty cardboard boxes should be kept to an absolute minimum and bins should be emptied regularly</li><li>Electrical equipment should be switched off when not in use for long periods</li><li>All electrical equipment must be tested for electrical safety at appropriate intervals</li><li>A fire alarm system must be installed, maintained and tested</li><li>Fire risk assessments should be carried out annually</li><li>All employees should be familiar with any fire routine procedures, for example, there should be regular fire drills so everyone knows their nearest fire exit and assembly point</li><li>Employees who smoke should only do so in designated areas</li><li>Fire exits should always be kept clear</li><li>Fire doors should not be held open</li></ul>
Working at height	<ul><li>Chairs or desks must not be used for reaching heights; step stools should be used instead</li><li>Staff should be trained in the proper use of ladders or other equipment that is used to reach heights, for example, fork lift truck</li></ul>
Hazardous substances	<ul><li>If any hazardous substances, for example, solvents or solvent-based glues are used within the office area, a risk assessment must be completed and employees should follow a safe system of work</li></ul>
Filing cabinets	<ul><li>Filing cabinets should be filled from the bottom up to maintain stability</li><li>Where filing cabinets are of the type that allows more than one drawer to be opened at a time, there should be a label warning of a risk of tipping</li><li>Drawers should be closed immediately after use</li><li>Filing cabinets should be positioned away from the door</li></ul>
Falling objects	<ul><li>Heavy items must not be stored on upper shelves – they should be stored at waist height.</li></ul>

DON'T FORGET

Risk assessments record the nature of the hazard, who might be harmed and how, what the organisation is already doing to prevent injury and what further action is necessary, who is responsible for taking the action and the deadline for carrying out the action.

DON'T FORGET

The Health and Safety Executive (HSE) is the national independent regulator that acts in the public interest to reduce work-related death and serious injury across Great Britain's workplaces. The HSE enforces all current health and safety legislation and provides information, advice and leaflets. These are available from their website www.hse.gov.uk

THINGS TO DO AND THINK ABOUT

Go to www.healthyworkinglives.com/advice/office-hazards and have a look at the advice given.

ACCIDENT REPORTING

RECORDING ACCIDENTS

Despite taking precautions, accidents do still happen and details of all accidents which result in an injury must be recorded in an **accident report book** or **accident report form**. Very serious accidents must also be reported to the Health and Safety Executive who will then carry out an investigation to find out exactly what happened. If the employer is found to be negligent they may be fined or may even be imprisoned.

When there is an accident, the following information is required to be recorded:

- full name, address and occupation of the person who was injured
- date and time of the accident
- place where the accident happened and a brief description of the circumstances
- nature of the injury
- details of any first aid treatment given
- name and address of any witnesses
- details of the person making the report and the time and date the report was made

EXAMPLE

Here is an example of an accident report form:

ABOUT THE PERSON WHO HAD THE ACCIDENT			
Name:		Date of Birth:	
Address:			
City/Town:	Postcode:	Telephone:	
Occupation:			
DETAILS OF PERSON REPORTING THIS ACCIDENT			
Name:			
Address:			
City/Town:	Postcode:	Telephone:	
Occupation:			
DETAILS OF ACCIDENT/INJURY			
Date:		Time:	
Where did the accident take place?			
Say how the accident happened, give a cause if you can			
Details of accident/injury:			
What first aid was given or other action taken?			
Name and address of any witnesses			
Signed:		Date:	
EMPLOYERS USE ONLY			
If this incident is reportable under RIDDOR (Reporting of Injuries, Diseases and Dangerous Occurrences Regulations 2013)			
How was it reported?			
Signed:		Date:	
Please note: to comply with the Data Protection Act 1998 personal details entered on accident report forms must be kept confidential.			

THINGS TO DO AND THINK ABOUT

Have a look at the office in the picture.
Make a list of any hazards that you can see.

SECURITY OF PEOPLE AND PROPERTY

SECURITY OF PEOPLE – USING IDENTIFICATION AND SECURE ENTRY SYSTEMS

It is important that people working in an organisation are kept safe and that no unauthorised persons can access the building. There are a number of measures that can be put in place and procedures that staff can follow to ensure that this does not happen:

- The organisation should install access control systems such as doors controlled by PIN codes or swipe cards or an intercom system. Doors such as these can be installed at the main entrance and at entrances to other areas around the building where access is restricted. Staff should ensure that these doors are always kept closed and they do not reveal PIN codes to others.

- Many organisations are now introducing biometric security systems. These use biometric technology to analyse biological information, for example, a fingerprint scanner which can identify a person by comparing a scan of the fingerprint against a database of prints. Many companies used specialised biometric security systems in conjunction with electronic locks to ensure that admittance to a room is restricted to people with appropriate clearance. Staff should be aware that the storage and use of biometric data meets the principles of the Data Protection Act 1998.

- Staff should be issued with ID badges which they should wear at all times.

- Staff may be required to use a Sign In/Out book every time they enter and leave the building. This will keep track of peoples' movements and can be used to identify any missing person in the event of a fire evacuation.

- Many organisations issue staff with a uniform not only to maintain a good company image, but also to identify who does and does not belong to the organisation. Staff must wear the uniform that they are issued with.

- All visitors to the organisation should report to Reception where they should give their name, the organisation they represent and the name of the person they have come to visit. In turn they will be given a numbered Visitors Badge which they should wear while on the premises. This information should be recorded in the Visitors Book along with a note of when the visitor returns the Visitors Badge and leaves the building at the end of their visit. Any member of staff receiving visitors should ensure such procedures are followed.

- The Reception area should never be left unattended and visitors should be accompanied by a member of staff at all times and should not be left to wander around on their own. Staff working in Reception must ensure they follow these policies.

- All staff should be trained to be vigilant to strangers and should report anyone they cannot identify. Reception staff should also be aware of suspicious parcels that may be left in Reception.

DON'T FORGET

The Data Protection Act 1998 creates rights for those who have their data stored and responsibilities for those who store, process or transmit such data. For example, any data that are held should be accurate and kept up to date.

SECURITY OF PROPERTY – FOLLOWING ORGANISATIONAL PROCEDURES TO PROTECT PROPERTY

It is important that property belonging to the organisation is kept secure and is not damaged or stolen. This is also true of property belonging to staff and visitors.

The following are examples of measures that the organisation can take to protect all property and the role that staff can play:

- Security guards can patrol the premises to prevent opportunist thieves and vandals entering the building. Staff should report any strangers so that the security guards can investigate.
- Lockable storage should be provided for personal belongings and staff should use the lockers that they are given.
- Staff should avoid bringing valuables and large amounts of money to work.
- Staff should ensure doors and windows are locked when they leave the premises at the end of the day.
- Security cables that have a lock should be used to attach computers and laptops to an immovable object. It might be possible to bolt equipment to desks.
- Equipment should be marked with an ultraviolet (UV) pen and a register of equipment serial numbers kept. This will help identify property in the event that it is stolen.
- CCTV should be installed to observe and record areas within and around the building, for example, the staff car park. Staff should monitor the CCTV screens for suspicious activity.
- The number of people who have keys to the building should be restricted and staff should take particular care not to lose keys. Any lost keys should be reported immediately.

- Security shutters operated with a PIN or special key to ensure only specific people can raise or lower them should be installed. Security shutters are often necessary for businesses that are likely to have high-value goods on their premises, as they are more likely to be burgled than other businesses. Staff should ensure that shutters are locked.
- Alarm systems can be installed to alert staff and the police to the presence of an intruder. In some situations, alarms that can be discretely activated by staff in an emergency are useful, for example, in banks and other locations that might be at risk of robbery.
- Security lights, that are either on constantly during the hours of darkness or that are motion activated, can be installed around the building to deter intruders.

THINGS TO DO AND THINK ABOUT

1. Biometric identification is now being used in airports – how is it being used?
2. What do you do at home and in school to ensure valuables are kept safe?

SECURITY OF INFORMATION

FOLLOWING ORGANISATIONAL PROCEDURES TO PROTECT PAPER AND ELECTRONIC INFORMATION

Of all the assets that a business owns, the one that is most vulnerable to security threats is the computer network; it is therefore vital that the network is protected from both internal and external threats. Hard copies of information must also be protected.

The following should be considered when storing information both manually and electronically:

- Staff should ensure that all paper documentation is accurately filed and stored in filing cabinets which should be locked if the information is confidential.

DON'T FORGET

Hard copy refers to paper documents and files stored in filing cabinets.

DON'T FORGET

As previously mentioned, the organisation has responsibilities to keep certain information secure under the Data Protection Act 1998.

- Staff should ensure that electronic documents are given appropriate names and stored in the correct folders within the computer system.
- A network connected to the internet is open to a whole host of potential problems such as viruses and malware and they can easily be downloaded by accident. Appropriate anti-virus software to protect against these threats should be installed and updated as necessary and the system should be scanned at regular intervals. Staff should ensure downloaded material is scanned before it is opened.
- Staff should not download games or any other programs from discs or the internet without permission.
- It is not just online threats from cyber space that can cause problems for the computer network. There are also many physical threats too, for example, if the main server was to lose power in the event of a power cut this could lead to masses of vital information being lost. It is therefore crucial that regular backups are taken and staff save their work at regular intervals throughout the day.
- Access to computer systems should be controlled by the use of logon IDs and passwords. Computer passwords should be changed at regular intervals and staff should not disclose their logon information or password to anyone.

- Access to folders or files can be restricted based on logon IDs and passwords, for example, in schools it is often the case that staff logon IDs allow access to folders not available to pupils. Staff should ensure they do not share their logon ID or password with anyone.
- Files that can be accessed by a number of users should be set up as 'read only' to prevent unauthorised changes being made.
- Staff should make use of encryption when sending confidential information. This means that the original message is scrambled but the receiving computer has a digital key to be able to work out the message.
- A record of who has access to confidential data should be kept and staff should consult this and follow procedures before disclosing personal information, for example, giving out an employee's salary information to a Supervisor.
- Staff should be aware that there can be no disclosure of confidential and sensitive information to others outside the organisation. Some organisations require employees to sign a confidentiality agreement as a condition of their employment.
- Staff should use a password-protected screensaver when they leave their computer for any length of time. This will prevent other people reading data on an unattended screen.
- Staff should be aware of their responsibilities and the law relating to hacking – there should be no unauthorised access to the system to change, steal or destroy information.
- Staff should follow procedures to dispose of out-of-date printouts, for example, by shredding.
- Restrictions may be in place as to what can be taken away from the office should staff want to work on a file at home and staff should be aware of this and their responsibilities for these files.

THINGS TO DO AND THINK ABOUT

Have a look at the following website which gives more information about computer hacking and predators: www.webroot.com/gb/en/home/resources/articles/pc-security/computer-security-threats-hackers

ORGANISING AND SUPPORTING SMALL-SCALE EVENTS

EVENTS ORGANISING 1

Businesses and other organisations are often involved in organising many different types of events, for example, monthly sales meetings involving sales personnel from other branches, a recruitment drive/careers evening, annual social events, charity fundraising events or new product launches. Running a successful event takes time, organisational skills and creativity, along with energy and enthusiasm.

Organising an event can be divided into three stages. At each stage, not only do a number of tasks have to be completed but a variety of documents and forms may have to be created or edited. Some events occur on a regular basis so the following may not always be relevant – however, even the most routine event can go wrong so always take time to double check that all arrangements are in place!

BEFORE THE EVENT

Know your aim and organise your team

- Know what kind of event you are organising and make sure your objectives are clear – establish your aims and the intended audience, including how many people you expect to attend.
- Put together a project team (if not to help before the event, certainly on the day).
- Plan out the work that has to be done and delegate – draw up a task list including when each task needs to be completed and who is doing it. Task lists and to-do lists can be stored electronically and updated as each task is completed and electronic reminders can be set. Make sure you have left yourself enough time to plan the event, for example, in the run up to Christmas, popular restaurants accept bookings in September which means there is no availability if you start to plan your Christmas party at the end of November!

Consider your budget

- Set the budget and decide how much money can be spent on the event. Costs can include items such as hire of the venue, catering, room decorations, entertainment, bringing in a speaker, printing and gifts. If you are hiring a venue you may need to pay a deposit. A spreadsheet can be set up to show a running total of all expenditure.
- As well as spending money you can plan how you are going to recover costs, for example, charge an entrance fee or sell refreshments. Find out if there is anyone who is willing to sponsor your event, particularly if it is a charity fundraising event. Again, this information can be added to the spreadsheet which should be updated regularly. Calculations can be included to show whether the event is being run within budget and, if not, action can be taken to ensure losses are kept to a minimum.

Think about your venue

- Carefully check out the venue. Not only do you have to take into consideration the cost of hiring the room but also the capacity and how it is laid out. Other considerations include: are tables and/or seating required? Are there other small rooms available nearby to store coats or where refreshments can be provided away from the main event? Is there wheelchair access? Are any special licences or permissions required?

- Very often a Room Booking form will have to be completed to ensure that the accommodation is reserved for your event and details of any special requirements are noted. One of the worst things that can happen is that the room is double-booked!

Prepare equipment and catering

- Think about what equipment is needed, for example, flipcharts, poster boards and AV equipment including digital projector and screen. This information might be included in the Room Booking form.
- Catering requirements have to be considered, for example, water being made available in a meeting room, tea/coffee/biscuits mid-morning, lunch and dinner. Think about different dietary requirements, for example, vegetarian or gluten-free options when planning menus, and remember to note catering costs in your spreadsheet. This information might also be included in your Room Booking form or there may be a separate Food/Beverage form.

Think about the risks

- Carry out a risk assessment and consider if there are any health and safety or security issues and what can be done to ensure there are no such problems. These can be noted down so that there is a record of what has been decided.

Consider the entertainment

- Decide on any entertainment that will be provided, for example, a band or DJ if it is a social function. If it is an information-giving event, decide if a speaker who has expertise in the subject should be invited – if so brief them as to the content of their talk and the length of time they should speak, give directions to the event and indicate whether you are paying any of their costs. Written confirmation may have to be sent detailing any arrangements that have been agreed to avoid confusion.

Ensure you have contacted attendees

- If you want people to come to your event you will need to tell them it is happening. Publicise the event by designing and creating posters to display on noticeboards, create flyers to advertise the event, send out invitations using mailing lists and make use of social media such as Facebook and Twitter. If the event is a business meeting then a Notice of Meeting and Agenda will have to be sent to attendees. See the section on Word Processing (p 66) for more on this.
- If you intend to charge people or limit the number of people who can attend, you will need to create tickets. Not only will the ticket have a number and the cost of the event but other relevant information such as date, time and venue.
  Any other documentation required for the event should be prepared well in advance, for example, multiple copies of a report required for a meeting, name badges for delegates and signage to direct people to the correct room.
- Immediately before the event ensure participants have all the information they require – travel directions to the event including maps, what the event is covering, catering and accommodation arrangements and a timetable of events. An itinerary could be drawn up to include this information. See the section on Word Processing (p 67) for more on this.

THINGS TO DO AND THINK ABOUT

Have a look at the following website: http://200svs.com/conference-events – the information is very comprehensive. Is there anything else you would like to know about this venue before you would decide to hold an event there?

EVENTS ORGANISING 2

ON THE DAY OF THE EVENT

Setting up the venue

- Set up the room in the layout required and check that any equipment is working and catering and refreshments are in place.
- Put up signs, for example, to direct those attending to the relevant room, or put up 'do not disturb' signs for any meetings.
- Make sure all helpers know the location of toilets, timings of breaks and lunch and have an emergency contact number that can be used to contact the event coordinator at any time.

Organising attendees and speakers

- If it is a conference or training session, register delegates as they arrive and have them sign an attendance sheet, give out name badges and issue any materials needed.
- Welcome and look after speakers or whoever is providing the entertainment.
- Have a final rehearsal if possible and check time schedules.
- As the event draws to a close, thank everyone for coming, including speakers and the audience, and make sure people know where they are going next, for example, if there is further catering or any transport arrangements.

Ask for feedback

- At the end of the event, issue feedback forms to those who have attended. Ask them to make comments about the event, how it was organised, the catering, accommodation and so on and to give any suggestions that might improve similar events in the future. You can use these feedback forms to eliminate any areas of weakness.

AFTER THE EVENT

- Immediately after the event tidy up the room, dispose of rubbish and ensure leftover food and drink is disposed of.
- Write to thank all speakers/entertainers for their contribution and keep them informed about expense payments.
- Ensure all outstanding invoices and bills are paid, for example, caterers and room hire.
- If the purpose of the event has been to raise money, tally up the amount achieved and publicise to those who have made a contribution. If the event was a meeting, prepare the Minutes of Meeting ready for the Chairperson's signature.
- Meet with all those involved in the organisation of the event to discuss how it went, what has been learned and what would be done differently next time. Remember to take into account any feedback received from those attending the event. An example of a feedback form is shown opposite.

EXAMPLE

Course Evaluation Form

We would like to obtain your input about this and future courses. Please help us by completing the following information.

1. Speaker's Presentation   ☐ Excellent   ☐ Good   ☐ Fair   ☐ Poor
   Comments: _____

2. Presentation Content: ☐ Excellent   ☐ Good   ☐ Fair   ☐ Poor
   Comments: _____

3. Was the presentation beneficial to you?   ☐ Yes   ☐ No
   Comments: _____

4. Did you receive the information you expected?   ☐ Yes   ☐ No
   Comments: _____

5. Was sufficient time provided for the presentation?   ☐ Yes   ☐ No
   Comments: _____

6. Accommodation: ☐ Excellent   ☐ Good   ☐ Fair   ☐ Poor
   Comments: _____

7. Catering/Refreshments: ☐ Excellent   ☐ Good   ☐ Fair   ☐ Poor
   Comments: _____

8. Please give any other comments you feel relevant:

   _____

   _____

THINGS TO DO AND THINK ABOUT

1. Have a look at the layouts given and decide which layouts might suit:
   (a) A retirement party
   (b) A lecture about health and safety in the office
   (c) Monthly sales planning meeting

Theatre

U-shape

Classroom

Boardroom

Banquet

Cabaret

2. Now that you know what is involved in organising and supporting an event, are there any events coming up in your school that you could help to run? For example, a fundraising non-uniform day – write down what you would do before the event, on the day of the event and after the event.

PRACTICE ASSIGNMENT

ADMINISTRATIVE PRACTICES

You work as an Administrative Assistant for Glendevon Electrical Installations, a small company which installs plasma TVs and sound systems. The company is expanding and they are looking to recruit and appoint another Administrative Assistant. Using your knowledge and skills complete the following tasks to support the recruitment process and assist Mr John Sim, Managing Director.

Print one copy of each task as you complete it. Remember to include your name in the document footer.

⊙ TASK 1

In order that you can easily find all your completed tasks, set up a folder in your My Documents called *GLENDEVON RECRUITMENT EVENT*.

⊙ TASK 2

To ensure the recruitment event runs smoothly, compile an electronic task list (you will find this facility in Outlook) and add the following tasks:

1 create stationery letterhead
2 prepare job advertisement
3 arrange interviews and enter appointments in diary
4 complete Customer Care information sheet to give to candidates
5 send letter of appointment to successful candidate

6 prepare standard letter to unsuccessful candidates
7 complete Health and Safety PowerPoint presentation to be shown on Induction Day
8 create Security information sheet
9 create Customer Survey form

Score each task off your list as you complete it.

⊙ TASK 3

Mr Sim has decided that the company should have a logo which will appear on all stationery from now on. Search the internet for a suitable image (similar to the one shown) and save it as *Glendevon Logo*.

⊙ TASK 4

Create a letterhead using the new logo and the company's contact details that will be used in the correspondence sent to applicants. Use a font of your choice and centre the details. Insert the logo at the top right-hand corner. In the centre of the page footer, add the text 'Visit us at www. glendevon.co.uk'. Save the letterhead as *Glendevon Letterhead*.

Glendevon Electrical Installations
Unit 4B
Canal Industrial Estate
Longton
FR6 9KL

Telephone: 07232 783920
E-mail: enquiries@glendevon.co.uk

TASK 5

The following job advertisement is to be placed in the local job centre and will also be published on Glendevon's website. Key in the advertisement and outline three tasks that the administrative assistant will carry out as well as three skills and qualities the successful candidate should have. Include the Glendevon logo at the top right-hand corner of the document. Save the advertisement as *Admin Assist Advert*.

> *Glendevon Electrical Installations*
>
> *We are currently looking for an enthusiastic and motivated Administrative Assistant to work in our busy office. This is a challenging and interesting position offering a lot of variety.*
>
> *Tasks and duties include:*
> -
>
> *While this position would suit a school leaver with a minimum of National 4 Administration and IT qualification, in addition the ideal candidate should display the following skills and qualities:*
> -
>
> *The hours of work are 9 am – 5 pm, Monday to Friday with one hour for lunch. Starting salary is competitive and we offer a generous holiday entitlement.*
>
> *More information about our company can be found at www.glendevon.co.uk*
>
> *Please reply in writing to Mr John Sim, Managing Director, Glendevon Electrical Installations, Unit 4B, Canal Industrial Estate, Longton, FR6 9KL or e-mail jsim@glendevon.co.uk*

➕ DON'T FORGET

Not sure how to layout a business letter? Have a look at pp 64–65.

 TASK 6

Two weeks after the advertisement has been placed in the job centre and online, there have been a total of 29 applications. Mr Sim has looked through all the letters and CVs he has received and has decided that he would like to interview three candidates next Friday morning. He would like to schedule the appointments at hourly intervals starting with Miss Samantha Jones at 9.30 am, then Mr Josh Hughes and finally Miss Kerry Ross. He has already telephoned Miss Jones and Miss Ross but he has been unable to contact Mr Hughes so a letter requesting that he attend for interview will have to be sent. Mr Hughes' address is 25 Park Crescent, Longton, FR2 7KL. The letter is shown here. Complete any missing information as appropriate. Save the letter as *Interview Letter*.

> Dear
>
> Interview for post of
>
> Further to your application for the above position we would like to invite you to attend for interview on   at   .
>
> Please telephone me on the above number to confirm your attendance or to make another suitable appointment.
>
> Yours etc.

 TASK 7

Enter the three interview appointments in your diary so that you can greet the candidates as they arrive. Also set an electronic reminder for 9.00 am on the morning of the interviews to check the layout of the meeting room and set up for tea/coffee.

➕ DON'T FORGET

Unsure of how to set up a bi-fold booklet? See pp 68–69.

 TASK 8

Customers are the lifeblood of an organisation and for Glendevon Electrical Installations this is no exception. In order that the candidates coming for interview are aware of how important this is, Mr Sim would like you to create a bi-fold booklet explaining how to achieve good customer service and what the benefits are. Save the booklet as *Customer Service Leaflet*.

FRONT PAGE

Use the same font that you used for the letterhead and remember to include our logo

Use a different font here, embolden and increase the font size

> *Glendevon Electrical Installations*
> *Unit 4B*
> *Canal Industrial Estate*
> *Longton*
> *FR6 9KL*
>
> **Our customers come first – a sale once lost is lost forever!**

INSIDE LEFT

Complete this page by outlining three features of good customer service

> When it comes to dealing with customers *EVERYONE* in our organisation plays an important role. You can help by:
> -
> -
> -

INSIDE RIGHT

Complete this page by outlining three benefits of providing good customer service

> By treating our customers in the best possible way we will benefit in the following ways:
> -
> -
> -

BACK PAGE

> The role of Administrative Assistant is crucial to our organisation – do you have the right skills and qualities? Are you the right person for the job? What contribution can you make to the business so that it is successful and grows?
>
> Are you the right person for the job?

ADMINISTRATIVE PRACTICES: PRACTICE ASSIGNMENT (CONTD.)

◎ TASK 9

Following the interviews it has been decided to offer Mr Hughes the job. Prepare the following letter of appointment. Remember to use the letterhead you created in Task 4. Save this letter as *Appointment Letter*.

Glendevon Electrical Installations
Unit 4B
Canal Industrial Estate
Longton
FR6 9KL

Telephone: 07232 783920
E-mail: enquiries@glendevon.co.uk

Dear

I hereby confirm our offer of the position of Administrative Assistant. This position is offered subject to satisfactory references and pre-employment checks and completion of a 4-week probationary period, during which time your performance will be reviewed.

Full details of hours of work, rate of pay, holiday entitlement, grievance and disciplinary procedures, etc. will be as discussed at your interview and will be stated in a Contract of Employment which will be issued to you within 6 weeks from your date of commencement.

Please find enclosed a Salary Payment Form which I would be grateful if you could complete and return to me as soon as possible.

We are all looking forward to working with you and hope you will soon feel part of the team. If you have any questions, please contact me.

Yours etc.

◎ TASK 10

The unsuccessful candidates who attended an interview must also receive a letter. Prepare a letter to Miss Samantha Jones, 16 Greendale Place, Longton, FR7 3TG and also one to Miss Kerry Ross, 83 Clayton Avenue, Longton, FR2 9AD. Save the letter as *Interview Letter 2*.

Glendevon Electrical Installations
Unit 4B
Canal Industrial Estate
Longton
FR6 9KL

Telephone: 07232 783920
E-mail: enquiries@glendevon.co.uk

Dear

Position of Administrative Assistant

Thank you for attending the interview in connection with the above vacancy. Unfortunately your application was not successful on this occasion. The calibre of all candidates was very high and, with your permission, we would like to keep your details on file so that we may contact you again should a similar vacancy arise in the near future.

In the meantime I would like to thank you for attending the interview and I wish you every success in the future.

Yours etc.

◎ TASK 11

In preparation for Josh starting with the company, prepare a brief presentation outlining what hazards he might encounter in the office and what he should do to make sure he works safely. Ensure you save your completed presentation as *Safety Presentation* so that it can be shown to future new recruits. Put the name of the company in the footer of all slides and print one copy in handout format showing six slides per page. Add a background, some animation and graphics to make the presentation interesting.

Slide 1 – Title slide layout

> **Health and safety – your responsibilities**

Slide 2 – Title and content layout

> **Hazards you might find in the workplace**
>
> List four hazards you might find in the workplace – bullet your list

Slide 3 – Title and content layout

> **What should you do to avoid accidents?**
>
> List four ways accidents in the office can be avoided – bullet your list

Slide 4 – Title and content layout

> **Accident Report Form – what should be included**
>
> Give details of information required in an Accident Report Form

Slide 5 – Title and content layout

> **Work safe – keep safe!**

DON'T FORGET

Unsure of how to add graphics or animation to your presentation? See pp 76–81.

◎ TASK 12

Prepare an information sheet about employees' responsibilities for security in relation to people, property and information which will be issued to Josh on the day he starts. Jim also thinks it would be a good idea if a copy is put on the staff noticeboard to serve as a reminder to existing staff.

Complete three bullet points under the headings People, Property and Information detailing what you think are the most important responsibilities. Include some relevant graphics to highlight your chosen points. Save the document as *Staff Security*.

◎ TASK 13

Jim would like to make sure all customers are happy. Create the following feedback form that engineers will give to customers when they complete the work they have been requested to do.

Start by using the letterhead you created in Task 4 and save the completed form as *Survey Form*.

Glendevon Electrical Installations
Unit 4B
Canal Industrial Estate
Longton
FR6 9KL

Telephone: 07232 783920
E-mail: enquiries@glendevon.co.uk

CUSTOMER SURVEY FORM

In order that we can provide the best possible service to all our customers, please help by giving your opinion of the service we have delivered.

Circle the appropriate number, where 1 is very good and 5 is very poor.

               1   2   3   4   5

1 How easy was it to make an appointment that suited you?

2 Did the engineer arrive on time?

3 Was the work completed to your satisfaction?

4 Did the engineer leave the work area tidy?

5 How likely are you to use our services again?

Please give any other comments you feel are relevant:

_____

_____

_____

Thank you for completing this survey.
We look forward to being of assistance to you again.

Visit us at www.glendevon.co.uk

SPREADSHEETS

AN OVERVIEW

USING SPREADSHEETS

A spreadsheet allows **calculations** to be performed and **graphs and charts** to be created. Spreadsheets are made up of rows and columns forming a grid of **cells**. Each row has a number and each column has a letter and this means that each **cell** has its own individual address.

EXAMPLE

For example, the address of this cell is **B2**.

This address is also shown in the **Name** box at the top of the worksheet.

Cells can contain text, numbers or formulae to carry out a calculation.

Spreadsheets use symbols within formulae similar to those you would use in maths:

Calculation	Symbol
Addition	+
Subtraction	-
Multiplication	*
Division	/

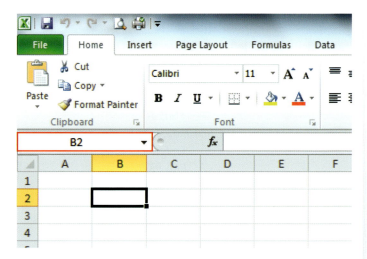

EXAMPLE

You want to find the value of sales for three items as well as the total sales of all items.

The calculation to find the total sales value of biscuits is 6 × £0.50 which will go in D4.

Using the cell addresses of these two numbers, the calculation used in the spreadsheet would be *=B4*C4*

You now want to do a similar calculation for crisps and then lemonade so copy the formula down the column – the computer will automatically change the row number as the formula is copied down.

In cell D7, you want to find the overall TOTAL value so the formula should be =D4+D5+D6. However, when adding a column or row of figures it is much more efficient to use the **AutoSum** button (Σ), which is found in the Home tab. The steps are: click in cell D7, click Σ and the computer will include all the required cells within the range so just press the return key or enter key. The formula now reads =SUM(D4:D6).

VALUE VIEW			
A	**B**	**C**	**D**
1 SALES			
2			
3 ITEM	QUANTITY	PRICE	TOTAL
4 Biscuits	6	£0.50	£3.00
5 Crisps	8	£0.35	£2.80
6 Lemonade	14	£0.60	£8.40
7 TOTAL			£14.20

FORMULAE VIEW			
A	**B**	**C**	**D**
1 SALES			
2			
3 ITEM	QUANTITY	PRICE	TOTAL
4 Biscuits	6	£0.50	=B4*C4
5 Crisps	8	£0.35	=B5*C5
6 Lemonade	14	£0.60	=B6*C6
7 TOTAL			=SUM(D4:D6)

DON'T FORGET

You must *ALWAYS* start your formula with the = sign

SPREADSHEET TABS

The tabs, menus and commands you are most likely to use are:

Home tab

This allows you to select **font** and **font size** and **styles** and format your spreadsheet including **text alignment**, **borders and shading**, **text wrapping** and **merging cells**. You can also **insert** and **delete rows and columns** and use **AutoSum** to add up a column of figures and to find **minimum**, **maximum**, **count numbers** and **average**.

Page Layout tab

This allows you to select various **print options** including **orientation**, **print area**, **gridlines and row and column headings** and **fit to one page** (see later)

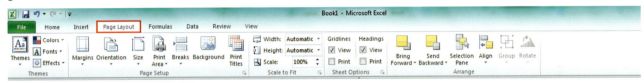

Formulas tab

Here you can **show formulas** used in your calculations

Data tab

This allows you to **sort** the information contained in your worksheet

Review tab

Here you can deal with **comments** included in the spreadsheet

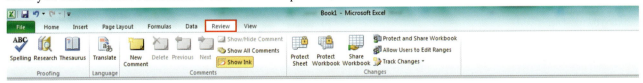

THINGS TO DO AND THINK ABOUT

Try making up a spreadsheet to work out your own financial situation for the next month. Add in all the money you expect to receive, for example, pocket money, wages from paper rounds, etc., then take away all the money you expect to spend and see how much you have left. Update your spreadsheet as the month goes on and where any of the amounts change!

COMMONLY USED FUNCTIONS 1

AUTOSUM

As well as keying in your own calculations, there are a number of calculations available to you from the AutoSum menu in the Home tab.

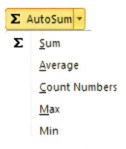

Sum will add numbers

Average will add the numbers then divide by the number of entries

Count Numbers will find out how many numerical entries are in the column or row

Max will find the highest number in the column or row

Min will find the lowest number in the column or row

Look at the example to see how these commonly used functions can be put into practice.

DON'T FORGET

Names are often split into two columns, for example, First Name and Surname, to allow sorting by surname.

DON'T FORGET

Count Numbers will NOT count names – only the number of **numerical** entries in a column/row. In this example, there is a Total mark against each name and this is what is being counted.

EXAMPLE

Value view

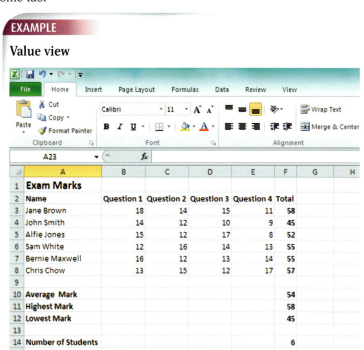

	A	B	C	D	E	F	G	H
1	**Exam Marks**							
2	**Name**	**Question 1**	**Question 2**	**Question 3**	**Question 4**	**Total**		
3	Jane Brown	18	14	15	11	58		
4	John Smith	14	12	10	9	45		
5	Alfie Jones	15	12	17	8	52		
6	Sam White	12	16	14	13	55		
7	Bernie Maxwell	16	12	13	14	55		
8	Chris Chow	13	15	12	17	57		
9								
10	**Average Mark**					54		
11	**Highest Mark**					58		
12	**Lowest Mark**					45		
13								
14	**Number of Students**					6		

Formula view

	A	B	C	D	E	F
1	**Exam Marks**					
2	**Name**	**Question 1**	**Question 2**	**Question 3**	**Question 4**	**Total**
3	Jane Brown	18	14	15	11	=SUM(B3:E3)
4	John Smith	14	12	10	9	=SUM(B4:E4)
5	Alfie Jones	15	12	17	8	=SUM(B5:E5)
6	Sam White	12	16	14	13	=SUM(B6:E6)
7	Bernie Maxwell	16	12	13	14	=SUM(B7:E7)
8	Chris Chow	13	15	12	17	=SUM(B8:E8)
9						
10	**Average Mark**					=AVERAGE(F3:F9)
11	**Highest Mark**					=MAX(F3:F8)
12	**Lowest Mark**					=MIN(F3:F8)
13						
14	**Number of Students**					=COUNT(F3:F8)

⊙ TASK: Addition, minimum, maximum, average and count

1 Create the following spreadsheet
2 Embolden and increase the size of the main heading
3 Embolden the column headings
4 Shade the last four rows
5 Enter a formula where you see ?
6 Put your name in the footer and save the exercise as Spreadsheet 1
7 Print on one page showing figures and gridlines (see p 30 for printing)
8 Print on one landscape page showing formulae and include gridlines and row and column headings

	A	B	C	D	E	F
1	**Exam marks**					
2	**First Name**	**Surname**	**Paper 1**	**Paper 2**	**Paper 3**	**Total Marks**
3	Sean	Smith	25	35	31	?
4	Hanna	Morris	26	25	21	?
5	Neil	Adams	23	20	24	?
6	David	Jones	25	28	29	?
7	Anthony	Black	28	27	25	?
8	Paula	McGill	28	29	25	?
9	Tara	McLean	26	22	23	?
10	Erin	Young	29	22	25	?
11	**Highest mark**		?	?	?	?
12	**Lowest mark**		?	?	?	?
13	**Average mark**		?	?	?	?
14	**Number of Students**		?			

COMMENTS

Comments can be added to cells within worksheets to give information or instructions to the operator. Using the Review tab, it is possible to add New Comments, Delete comments and Show or Hide comments. Very often you will have to use spreadsheets that contain comments which are your instructions.

➕ DON'T FORGET

ALWAYS use your mouse to point and click on the cells you want to include in your calculation rather than keying in cell references – you will be less likely to make a mistake!

➕ DON'T FORGET

When using the same formula on every row double click on the little black square at the bottom right of the cell on the first row – this will copy the formula down to the end of the column.

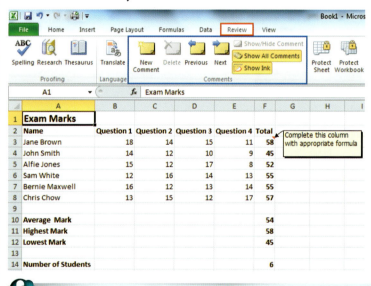

⊙ TASK: Multiplication

1 Create the following spreadsheet
2 Embolden and increase the size of the main heading
3 Embolden the column headings
4 Enter a formula in cell D3 then copy this formula down to cell D9

	A	B	C	D
1	**SNACKS**			
2	**Item**	**Selling price**	**Quantity sold**	**Total income**
3	Toasted sandwich	£1.20	20	?
4	Muffin	£0.40	4	?
5	Apple turnover	£0.25	6	?
6	Cookie	£0.20	5	?
7	Carrot cake	£0.65	10	?
8	Milk shake	£0.70	2	?
9	Fruit smoothie	£0.60	9	?

5 Put your name in the footer and save the exercise as Spreadsheet 2
6 Print on one page showing figures and gridlines
7 Print on one page showing formulae and include gridlines and row and column headings

💭 THINGS TO DO AND THINK ABOUT

Always ensure that you use appropriate and consistent formats. For example, money values should be set as currency – DO NOT KEY IN £. Also think about how many decimal places you want to show.

Use these buttons in the Home tab to adjust the number of decimal places.

To shade a cell:

COMMONLY USED FUNCTIONS 2

PRINTING YOUR SPREADSHEET

Spreadsheets can be printed either showing values or showing formulae. Printing values will show you the **answers** to your calculations expressed in numbers. Printing in formula view will show **how** the calculation has been carried out. To show the formula, click on Show Formulas button which is available in the Formulas tab.

A formula can often take up a lot of space within the column, so before you print you must ensure that all of the formula can be seen and that it is not cut off or truncated.

Widening the columns means that prints can go over two pages or more. Therefore, it is important to use the **Fit to** facility within the **Page Setup** dialogue box that will automatically shrink the spreadsheet to fit onto one page.

In addition, when printing formulae you will often be asked to print the gridlines and the row and column headings at the same time – printing these makes it easier to check exactly which cells have been used in your calculations. Buttons for these are available in the Page Layout tab but there are also options within the **Page Setup** dialogue box.

EXAMPLE

This example shows formulae that have been truncated:

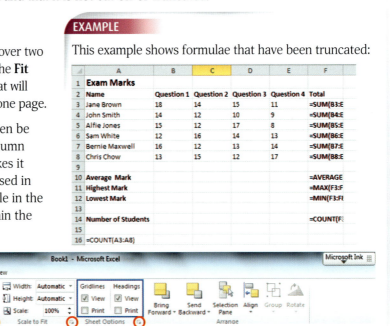

The **Page Setup** dialogue box is one of the most-used dialogue boxes in Excel when it comes to printing your work and it can be opened from any of the dialogue box launcher buttons in the Page Layout tab.

Page tab will allow you to choose Orientation and Fit to 1 page wide by 1 page tall

Margins tab will allow you to change margins and centre the spreadsheet on the page

Header/Footer tab will allow you to enter information into the document's header or footer

Sheet tab will allow you to print gridlines as well as row and column headings. If your spreadsheet has comments then you can choose if, and where, you want them printed

The **Page Setup** dialogue box is also available from File, Print

PRACTICAL TASKS

Now try some of these exercises which will test your knowledge of using calculations within spreadsheets as well as formatting cells, shading and bordering and sorting.

ONLINE

For more practical tasks, head to www.brightredbooks.net/N5AdminIT

⊙ TASK: Subtraction and sorting

1 Create the following spreadsheet
2 Embolden and increase the size of the main heading
3 Embolden the column headings
4 Enter a formula where you see ?
5 **Sort the spreadsheet in ascending order of Net Cost**
6 Put your name in the footer and save the exercise as Spreadsheet 3
7 Print on one page showing figures and gridlines
8 Print on one page showing formula and include gridlines and row and column headings

	A	B	C	D
1	**CITY BREAKS**			
2	**Destination**	**Cost**	**Discount**	**Net cost**
3	Paris	£500	£50	?
4	Rome	£550	£25	?
5	Athens	£600	£75	?
6	London	£375	£25	?
7	Madrid	**£480**	**£30**	?
8	New York	**£1200**	**£125**	?

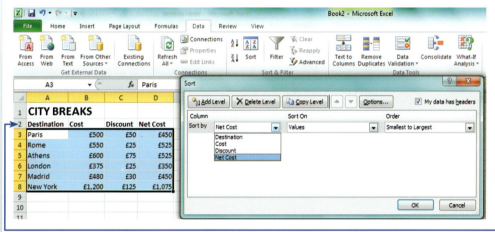

DON'T FORGET

Be very careful when sorting in a spreadsheet. You must select **all** the information you want included in the sort, otherwise only one column will be sorted and that information will no longer match the remaining information in the row.

JUST A WEE NOTE

The headings in row 2 of the spreadsheet have been included in the selection (they are just not shaded here). This makes it easier to choose which column to sort in the Sort dialogue box.

⊙ TASK: Division, sorting and text wrapping

1 Create the following spreadsheet
2 Embolden and increase the size of the main heading
3 Embolden the column headings and **wrap the text**
4 Enter a formula where you see ?
5 **Sort the spreadsheet in descending order of Price per person**
6 Put your name in the footer and save the exercise as Spreadsheet 4
7 Print on one page showing figures and gridlines
8 Print on one page showing formula and include gridlines and row and column headings

	A	B	C	D
1	**FAMILY HOLIDAYS**			
2	**Destination**	**Total cost**	**Number in family**	**Price per person**
3	Florida	£3650	5	?
4	Cyprus	£2895	5	?
5	Majorca	£1500	4	?
6	Lanzarote	£1800	4	?
7	Greece	£2000	5	?
8	Portugal	£900	3	?

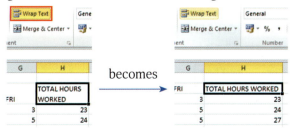

becomes

DON'T FORGET

Text wrapping allows you to put all the words in one cell on more than one line. Wrap Text can be found in the Home tab. Note that occasionally you have to adjust the column widths/depths to allow text wrapping to take effect.

DON'T FORGET

The symbol you will need for division is /

CHARTING

It is very easy to create charts and graphs using the data stored in a spreadsheet.
Various different types of chart are available from the Insert tab.

COLUMN CHART

Column charts are used when you want to *compare different values vertically side-by-side*. Each column represents the value for one piece of data.

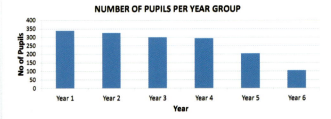

PIE CHART

Pie charts *show values as a percentage of the whole*. Different colours are used to to represent each item.

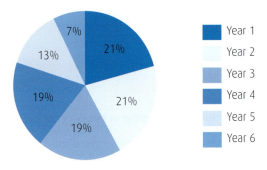

BAR CHART

Bar charts are like column charts but they *compare different values horizontally*.

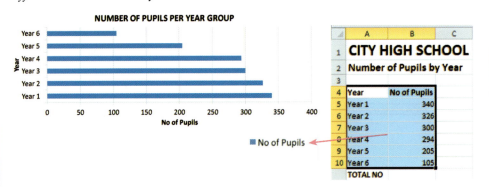

LINE GRAPH

Line graphs are used to *illustrate trends over a period of time*. Each value is plotted and is connected to the next value by a line.

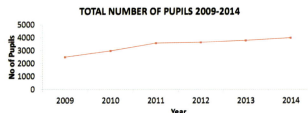

DON'T FORGET

Always include a Chart Title and label both the horizontal and the vertical axes. The legend is not always relevant – think carefully if you need a *key* to explain what each colour represents.

DON'T FORGET

To create a chart using columns in different parts of the worksheet select the first column then hold down the control key [ctrl] and select the second column.

DON'T FORGET

When creating a chart be careful to only select the information you want plotted in your chart – not all information should be included. *Including the column heading in your selection automatically creates a legend.*

CHART TOOLS

Once you have created your chart more options become available under **Chart Tools**

The *Design* tab will let you Move Chart to a separate sheet

The *Layout* tab will let you add a Chart Title, Axis Titles, Legend and specify Data Labels

PRACTICAL EXERCISES

Now try some of these exercises which will test your knowledge of creating charts within a spreadsheet.

⊙ TASK: Column Chart

Compare the test marks of pupils in English class.

1 Enter the data below into a spreadsheet

	A	B
1	**TEST RESULTS – ENGLISH**	
2	**Name**	**Mark**
3	Danielle Dempsey	25
4	Hannah Coole	56
5	Declan Taylor	63
6	Jamie Methven	45
7	Paul Wood	58
8	Carrie Gill	76

2 Create a **column chart** using the chart wizard
3 Chart title: **TEST RESULTS – ENGLISH**
4 Label the X axis: **Name**
5 Label the Y axis: **Mark**
6 **Do NOT include the legend**
7 Put the chart into a **new sheet**
8 Put your name in the footer
9 Save the spreadsheet as **Chart 1**
10 Print one copy of your chart

THINGS TO DO AND THINK ABOUT

Focus Fashions wishes to compare sales between its departments for the month of April.

1. Enter the data below into a spreadsheet

	A	B
1	SALES	
2	DEPARTMENT	APRIL SALES (£m)
3	Shoes	£2345
4	Womenswear	£3345
5	Menswear	£2800
6	Childrenswear	£3015
7	Accessories	£485

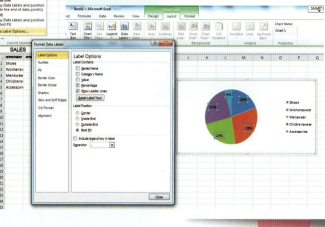

2. Create a **pie chart**
3. Pie chart title: **APRIL SALES (£m)**
4. **Label your pie chart with the percentage sales – to do this go to Layout tab then Data Labels then More Data Label Options .... The Format Data Labels dialogue box will open so click on Percentage**
5. **Ensure your legend indicates the departments**
6. Put the chart into a **new sheet**
7. Put your name in the footer
8. Save the spreadsheet as **Chart 3**
9. Print one copy of your pie chart

ONLINE

For tasks on charting, head to www.brightredbooks.net/ N5AdminIT

EXTENSION: ABSOLUTE CELL REFERENCES

RELATIVE AND ABSOLUTE CELL REFERENCING

When you carry out a calculation in a spreadsheet and want to do the same calculation in the following rows, copy the formula down the column and the cell references will be changed automatically.

EXAMPLE

VALUE VIEW			
	A	**B**	**C**	**D**
1	SALES			
2				
3	ITEM	QUANTITY	PRICE	TOTAL
4	Biscuits	6	£0.50	£3.00
5	Crisps	8	£0.35	£2.80
6	Lemonade	14	£0.60	£8.40
7	TOTAL			£14.20

FORMULAE VIEW			
	A	**B**	**C**	**D**
1	SALES			
2				
3	ITEM	QUANTITY	PRICE	TOTAL
4	Biscuits	6	£0.50	=B4*C4
5	Crisps	8	£0.35	=B5*C5
6	Lemonade	14	£0.60	=B6*C6
7	TOTAL			=SUM(D4:D6)

In each row of column D, the same calculation is being carried out: Total = Quantity × Price. When the formula is copied down from row 4 to row 5 to row 6, the cell references **automatically change**. This is known as **relative cell referencing**.

There are, however, occasions when you DO NOT WANT the cell references to change as they are copied – this is known as **absolute cell referencing**.

EXAMPLE

ALL items have 10% tax to be added

This amount and a text label to explain this figure is inserted two rows below the data

The 10% sales tax is the same for **all** items so you do not want cell reference B10 to change as the formula is copied down the column. When keying in the formula, immediately after pointing and clicking on cell B10, press the F4 key at the top of your keyboard to ensure this does not happen.

	A	B	C	D	E	F
1	SALES TAX					
2						
3	ITEM	QUANTITY	PRICE	TOTAL	TAX	TOTAL INCL TAX
4	Biscuits	6	£0.50	£3.00	£0.30	£3.30
5	Crisps	8	£0.35	£2.80	£0.28	£3.08
6	Lemonade	14	£0.60	£8.40	£0.84	£9.24
7	TOTAL			£14.20		
8						
9						
10	Sales Tax	10%				

The formula will now be =D4*B10. The $ sign around cell reference B10 means that cell reference WILL NOT CHANGE as it is copied. However, D4 will still change to D5 then D6.

	A	B	C	D	E	F
1	SALES TAX					
2						
3	ITEM	QUANTITY	PRICE	TOTAL	TAX	TOTAL INCL TAX
4	Biscuits	6	£0.50	=B4*C4	=D4*B10	=D4+E4
5	Crisps	8	£0.35	=B5*C5	=D5*B10	=D5+E5
6	Lemonade	14	£0.60	=B6*C6	=D6*B10	=D6+E6
7	TOTAL			=SUM(D4:D6)		
8						
9						
10	Sales Tax	10%				

THINGS TO DO AND THINK ABOUT

Now try some of these exercises which will test your knowledge of using absolute cell references in spreadsheet calculations as well as formatting cells, shading and bordering and sorting.

DON'T FORGET

Remember to use the F4 key when clicking on the cell that will not change as the formula is copied down the column – in this exercise it is cell B8

TASK 1

1. Create the following spreadsheet
2. Embolden and increase the size of the main heading
3. Embolden the column headings and wrap the text
4. Enter a formula where you see **?**
5. Put your name in the footer and save the exercise as Absolute 1
6. Print on one page showing figures and gridlines
7. Print on one page showing formula and include gridlines and row and column headings

	A	B	C
1	**HOLIDAY BOOKINGS TO MAJORCA**		
2	**Family**	**Number in Party**	**Total Cost of Holiday**
3	Gibson	5	?
4	Kilday	3	?
5	Baird	4	?
6	Dhillon	6	?
7			
8	Price per person	£352	

TASK 2

1. Create the following spreadsheet
2. Embolden and increase the size of the main heading
3. Embolden the column headings and wrap the text
4. Enter a formula where you see **?**
   Remember to use the F4 key where appropriate
5. Put your name in the footer and save the exercise as Absolute 2
6. Print on one page showing figures and gridlines
7. Print on one page showing formula and include gridlines and row and column headings

	A	B	C	D
1	**PETROL EXPENSE CLAIMS**			
2	**Initial**	**Surname**	**Number of Litres**	**Total Cost of Petrol Claimed**
3	J	Carter	62	?
4	S	Alison	45	?
5	H	James	57	?
6	D	Gizzi	53	?
7				
8	Price per litre		£1.32	

ONLINE

For a further task on absolute cell referencing, head to www.brightredbooks.net/N5AdminIT

TASK 3

1. Create the following spreadsheet
2. Embolden and increase the size of the main heading
3. Embolden the column headings and wrap the text
4. Enter a formula where you see **?**
   Remember to use the F4 key where appropriate
5. Put your name in the footer and save the exercise as Absolute 3
6. Print on one page showing figures and gridlines
7. Print on one page showing formula and include gridlines and row and column headings

	A	B	C	D	E
1	**COMMISSION EARNED**				
2	**Sales person**	**Sales**	**Commission Due**		**Commission**
3	Allan, W	£104,520	?		7.5%
4	Burns, C	£97,600	?		
5	Lister, F	£93,750	?		
6	Duncan, L	£102,690	?		
7	Ali, S	£99,570	?		
8	Zinaid, P	£101,750	?		

NAMING CELLS

CHANGING THE NAME OF A CELL

Cells in a spreadsheet are normally referenced according to their column and row. However, it is possible to change the name of a cell to make it more meaningful.

The Sales Tax of 10% is in cell **B10**.

To change this name, click in the name box, delete B10 and insert the words Sales_Tax (the computer will not accept a space between words so use _) and press the enter key or return key.

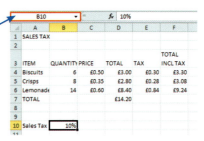

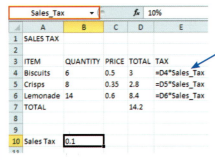

Now when a formula is inserted, the name of the cell will be included and not the cell reference. When the formula is copied down the named cell will remain unchanged, the same as using an absolute cell reference!

Got the cell name wrong? Go to the Formulas tab then click on Name Manager. Delete the name you don't want and go through the cell naming process again.

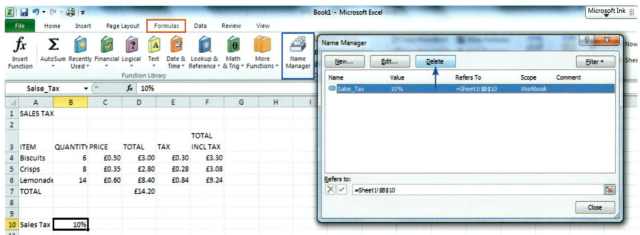

PRACTICAL EXERCISES

Now try the previous exercises but this time use named cells rather than pressing F4 and using absolute cell references. If you have already saved the exercises just delete the formula and input new formula.

⊙ TASK 1

1 Create the following spreadsheet
2 Embolden and increase the size of the main heading
3 Embolden the column headings and wrap the text
4 **Name cell B8 Price_Per_Person**
5 Enter a formula where you see ?
6 Put your name in the footer and save the exercise as Named 1
7 Print on one page showing figures and gridlines
8 Print on one page showing formula and include gridlines and row and column headings

	A	B	C
1	**HOLIDAY BOOKINGS TO MAJORCA**		
2	Family	Number in party	Total cost of holiday
3	Gibson	5	?
4	Kilday	5	?
5	Baird	4	?
6	Dhillon	4	?
7			
8	Price per person	£352	

ONLINE

For more tasks about naming cells, head to www. brightredbooks.net/N5AdminIT

TASK 2

1 Create the following spreadsheet
2 Embolden and increase the size of the main heading
3 Embolden the column headings and wrap the text
4 **Name cell B8 Petrol_Price**
5 Enter a formula where you see **?**
6 Put your name in the footer and save the exercise as Named 2
7 Print on one page showing figures and gridlines
8 Print on one page showing formula and include gridlines and row and column headings

	A	B	C
1	**PETROL EXPENSE CLAIMS**		
2	**Name**	**Number of Litres**	**Total Cost of Petrol Claimed**
3	Carter, J	62	?
4	Alison, S	45	?
5	James, H	57	?
6	Gizzi, D	53	?
7			
8	Price Per Litre	£1.32	

ANOTHER USE FOR NAMED CELLS...

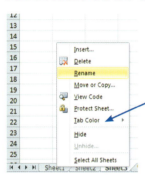

When you open a new Excel file you will notice that it contains three pages or worksheets for you to work with – they are named Sheet1, Sheet2 and Sheet3. To make the name of the worksheet more meaningful, right click on the sheet tab, select Rename and key in an appropriate title. You can also change the Tab Colour.

Often spreadsheet files are set up with a number of worksheets in use and information from one spreadsheet is used by another. When this happens it is often useful to 'name' the cell containing the information you want to copy over from one worksheet to the other.

EXAMPLE

There are two worksheets in use – one called **SALES** and one called **SUMMARY**

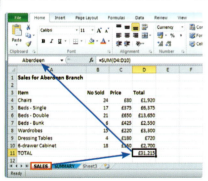

Cell D11 in the **SALES** worksheet has been named **Aberdeen**. This information is required in the **SUMMARY** worksheet

To insert this information into the **SUMMARY** worksheet click on cell B9 where you want the information to go, key in = then point and click on the **SALES** worksheet cell D11 which has been named **Aberdeen** and press the return or enter key.

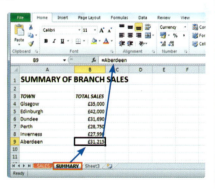

The information should now appear in cell B9 of the **SUMMARY** worksheet and the cell name will appear in the formula bar.

THINGS TO DO AND THINK ABOUT

1. Open a new spreadsheet file and **rename Sheet1 SALES**
2. Key in the data below. Embolden the main heading and the column headings
3. Enter a formula where you see **?**
4. **Name cell D11 Aberdeen – this figure is the total sales for the Aberdeen Branch and this information is required in the summary worksheet**

	A	B	C	D
1	**Sales for Aberdeen Branch**			
2				
3	**Item**	**No Sold**	**Price**	**Total**
4	Chairs	24	£80	?
5	Beds – Single	17	£375	?
6	Beds – Double	21	£650	?
7	Beds – Bunk	6	£425	?
8	Wardrobes	15	£220	?
9	Dressing Tables	4	£180	?
10	6-drawer Cabinet	18	£150	?
11	TOTAL			?

IF STATEMENTS

An IF formula will check if a cell entry is true or false and then give the appropriate answer. For example, the exam results for an English class are shown below in a spreadsheet. If a pupil achieves a mark of more than 50 then they have passed the exam; otherwise they have failed. An IF statement can be used to show this automatically.

VALUE VIEW		
A	**B**	**C**
1 ENGLISH MARKS		
2		
3 Name	Mark	Pass or Fail?
4 John Brown	65	Pass
5 Jill Smith	47	Fail
6 Tony Grant	68	Pass
7 Jordan Gray	50	Fail
8 Simon Jones	49	Fail

FORMULAE VIEW		
A	**B**	**C**
1 ENGLISH MARKS		
2		
3 Name	Mark	Pass or Fail?
4 John Brown	65	=IF(B4>50,"Pass","Fail")
5 Jill Smith	47	=IF(B5>50,"Pass","Fail")
6 Tony Grant	68	=IF(B6>50,"Pass","Fail")
7 Jordan Gray	50	=IF(B7>50,"Pass","Fail")
8 Simon Jones	49	=IF(B8>50,"Pass","Fail")

TO CREATE AN IF STATEMENT

Setting up an IF formula is very straightforward using a wizard. Start by clicking on f_x to open the **Insert Function** dialogue box. Within the **Select a function** menu select IF.

The IF wizard will now open.

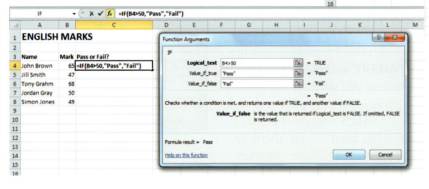

Logical test

With your mouse, click on the cell containing the variable information then key in the criteria. *In this example it is the cell containing the mark achieved by John Brown (cell B4) and the criteria is the pass mark of **more than 50***

Value if true

Key in the response should the cell match the criteria. *If John Brown's mark is more than 50 he achieves a "Pass"*

Value if false

Key in the response if the cell **does not** match the criteria. *If John Brown's mark is 50 or less he achieves a "Fail"*

Now click on OK.

Remember each person's mark is different so this is the variable information. The pass mark of more than 50 will determine whether or not the pupil has passed – this is the criteria. Complete each line of the wizard as follows:

DON'T FORGET

Always start by clicking on a cell then use one of these mathematical symbols in the first line of the wizard:

Symbol	Meaning
=	Equal to
<	Less than
<=	Less than or equal to
>	Greater than
>=	Greater than or equal to

Once the IF formula for the first person has been entered copy the formula down the column to calculate pass or fail for the remaining students.

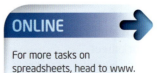

ONLINE

For more tasks on spreadsheets, head to www.brightredbooks.net/N5AdminIT

THINGS TO DO AND THINK ABOUT

Your challenge – copy the example above into a spreadsheet and try using the IF formula wizard for yourself. Check your IF formula carefully against the solution shown.

Now try these tasks which will test your knowledge of using an IF statement within a spreadsheet.

TASK 1

1. Create the following spreadsheet
2. Embolden and increase the size of the main heading
3. Embolden the column headings and wrap the text
4. **In cell D3 enter a formula which will show 'Profit' if Sales are more than Costs. Otherwise, the answer will be 'Loss'. Is your answer the same as this?**

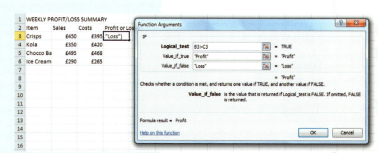

	A	B	C	D
1	**WEEKLY PROFIT/LOSS SUMMARY**			
2	**Item**	**Sales**	**Costs**	**Profit or Loss?**
3	Crisps	£450	£395	?
4	Kola	£350	£420	?
5	Chocco Bars	£495	£468	?
6	Ice Cream	£290	£265	?

5. Copy this formula down for the remaining three items
6. Put your name in the footer and save the exercise as IF 1
7. Print on one page showing figures and gridlines
8. Print on one page showing formula and include gridlines and row and column headings

TASK 2

1. Create the following spreadsheet
2. Embolden and increase the size of the main heading
3. Embolden the column headings and wrap the text
4. **In cell C3 enter a formula which will show £10 if the member is a Junior and £20 if the member is a senior. *Hint: you will need to use " " around the word in the first line of the formula wizard***

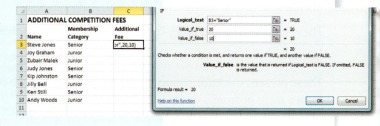

	A	B	C
1	**ADDITIONAL COMPETITION FEES**		
2	**Name**	**Membership Category**	**Additional Fee**
3	Steve Jones	Senior	?
4	Joy Graham	Junior	?
5	Zubair Malek	Junior	?
6	Judy Jones	Senior	?
7	Kip Johnston	Senior	?
8	Jilly Bell	Junior	?
9	Ken Still	Senior	?
10	Andy Woods	Junior	?

5. Copy this formula down for the remaining members
6. Format column C for currency to 0 decimal points
7. Put your name in the footer and save the exercise as IF 4
8. Print on one page showing figures and gridlines
9. Print on one page showing formula and include gridlines and row and column headings

DATABASES

USING DATABASES 1

Databases store large amounts of information in an organised and logical way. Data can be edited, updated or deleted but, more importantly, finding specific information and sorting information into a particular order is very quick and easy. Furthermore, data can be imported into other applications, for example, merging a letter created in Word with names and addresses saved in a database.

DATABASE OBJECTS

Database software, such as Access, consists of a number of objects within a database file. The objects we are concerned with are:

Tables

These contain all the information or data about a particular subject, for example, names, addresses, telephone number and date of birth of pupils.

Tables are made up of **records** and each record is divided into **fields**.

- A **record** is information about one person or one thing.
- A **field** is a single item of information about a person or thing that appears in every record, for example, all surnames are held within the Surname field. Putting different types of information into different fields makes it easier to sort and to search for specific information.

Fields can be **formatted** for text, date, currency, number/auto number or yes/no.

Queries

These are searches carried out on tables to find specific information, for example, to find all pupils with the surname Smith.

Forms

These can be set up to make it easier to input information into a table.

Reports

These present the information in a particular way and are produced either directly from a table or from a query.

DON'T FORGET

Tables, queries, forms and reports can all be saved to be accessed at a later date – make sure you use relevant names for each object.

DATABASE TABS

The tabs, menus and commands you are most likely to use are:

- *Home* tab – allows you to change **View** from Datasheet View to Design View, **sort** a field as well as select **font** and **font size** and **style**.

- *Create* tab – allows you to **Design a Query** and create **Forms** and **Reports** using **Wizards**.

- *External Data* – use this tab when you want to **print your table** or **Query**. Click on More then select Word. In the Export–RTF File dialogue box, ensure you select the option to open the destination file before clicking OK. Your database table will now open in a Word document and you can insert your name in the footer.

DON'T FORGET

In Word you can right click on the table and select AutoFit to Window to ensure all the data are visible.

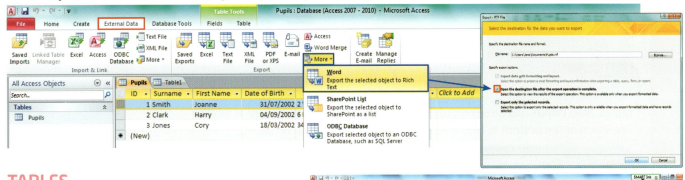

TABLES

It is important to note that Access always wants to save any changes. Even before you start to work on your database you first have to give your **file** a name and save it. Clicking on Create will open a new **table** in Datasheet view. You must also give your **table** a name when you have finished creating it.

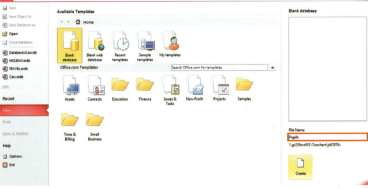

When the table opens in **Datasheet View**, you can start to set up **fields** – this is how your information is grouped. It is often a good idea to think about whether you will want to sort or query on a specific piece of information, for example, sort by surname. If so, then there should be a field containing only surnames. In addition, fields should be formatted according to the information contained within them; for example, text or date or number or currency.

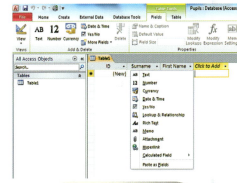

When you *Click to Add* a new field first select format then key in the field name. Add as many fields as you will need.

Note that Access 2010 will automatically give you an **ID** field which is formatted as **AutoNumber** – this means that the computer will automatically number records as you add them to your table. This field is also set up as a **primary key**. A primary key contains information that is unique to each record – it is impossible to use that same information in any other record in the table; for example, each student will have an ID number which cannot be used for any other pupil in the table. You can delete this field if you do not require it.

DON'T FORGET

Select the format of the field here, for example, dates can be long, medium or short.

THINGS TO DO AND THINK ABOUT

To make any changes to a field, for example, change format, rename, delete or add a field once the table has been created, click on the View button and switch to **Design View** and make your changes. Clicking again on the View button will take you back to the **Datasheet View** of your table where you can start to enter your **records**. (You will notice that as soon as you change the way you view your table, you will be asked to save!)

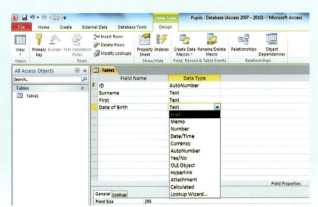

USING DATABASES 2

TABLES (CONTD)

EXAMPLE

Here is an example of a database table shown in **Datasheet View**. This database table called **Pupils** has three records and eight fields. Notice that there is a blank line given at the bottom of the table ready for a new record to be added.

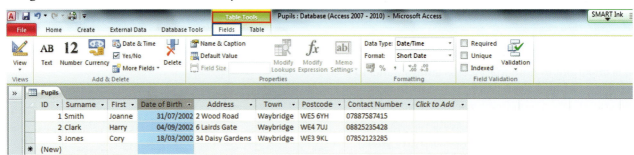

Notice that Table Tools are available in Datasheet View. Under the Fields tab it is possible to amend formats, delete fields and make other changes to fields just as you would in Design View.

THINGS TO DO AND THINK ABOUT

Now try some of these exercises which will test your knowledge of setting up a database table, **sorting** the information within the table, editing and deleting records and printing.

TASK 1

1. Create a database file called **Pupil Information**. Within this file create a database table called **Pupils** and use the field names and field formats listed below:

FIELD NAME	FIELD FORMAT
ID	AutoNumber
Surname	Text
First Name	Text
Date of Birth	Date – short date
Address	Text
Town	Text
Postcode	Text
Contact Number	Text

2. Add the following records:

Surname	First Name	Date of Birth	Address	Town	Postcode	Contact Number
Smith	Joanne	31/07/02	2 Wood Road	Waybridge	WE5 6YH	07887587415
Clark	Harry	04/09/02	6 Lairds Gate	Waybridge	WE4 7UJ	08825235428
Jones	Cory	18/03/02	34 Daisy Gardens	Waybridge	WE3 9KL	07852123285

3. **Sort** the database into ascending order of Surname
4. **Print** one copy of your table in Datasheet View – ensure you put your name in the footer of your printout.

DON'T FORGET

Double click with your mouse between the field headings to adjust column widths so that data are not truncated. The column is not wide enough if you see #######

DON'T FORGET

This field will be included automatically.

DON'T FORGET

Postcodes containing a mix of numbers and letters and telephone numbers beginning with '0' must both be formatted as **text**.

DON'T FORGET

To **sort on one field** within a Table click on the field name then select either the Ascending (A to Z) or Descending (Z to A) button in the Home tab.

TASK 2

1. Create a database file called **Holiday Bookings** and a database table called **Holidays**. Use the field names and field formats listed below:

FIELD NAME	FIELD FORMAT
ID	AutoNumber
Title	Text
First Name	Text
Surname	Text
Holiday Destination	Text
Cost of Holiday	Currency – 0 decimal points
Deposit Paid	Yes/No
Date of Departure	Date – short date
Number of Nights	Number

2. Add the following records:

Title	First Name	Surname	Holiday Destination	Cost of Holiday	Deposit Paid	Date of Departure	No of Nights
Mr	John	Fallon	Corfu	£500	Yes	26/04/2015	7
Mrs	Joan	Green	Majorca	£875	Yes	26/05/2015	10
Mr	William	Donald	Crete	£1,090	No	14/07/2015	14
Mr	Joe	Wilson	Ibiza	£450	No	01/06/2015	10
Mr	Steven	Thomson	Majorca	£382	Yes	14/07/2015	7
Ms	Susan	Ballantyne	Ibiza	£475	Yes	25/06/2015	10

3. **Sort** the database into ascending order of Number of Nights
4. **Print** one copy of your table in Datasheet View – ensure you put your name in the footer of your printout.

TASK 3

1. Create a database file called **Students** and a table called **Student Information**. Use the field names and field formats listed below:

FIELD NAME	FIELD FORMAT
ID	AutoNumber
First Name	Text
Surname	Text
Street	Text
Town	Text
Postcode	Text
Year of Study	Number
Date of Birth	Date – long
Leaver	Yes/No

2. Add the following records

First Name	Surname	Street	Town	Postcode	Year of Study	Date of Birth	Leaver
Julie	Williams	21 Hope Street	Newtown	NW4 7YH	2	19/03/1994	No
James	Farr	31 Pine Road	Northwich	NH4 8UJ	4	14/08/1992	Yes
Greg	Fawls	71 Loch Tay Drive	Newtown	NW3 6KL	3	28/02/1992	Yes
Fiona	Anderson	20 Scott Way	Northwich	NH3 8WS	3	19/05/1992	Yes
Peter	Parker	67 South Street	Newtown	NW9 7TF	1	27/04/1993	No
Paula	Bruce	92 High Street	Northwich	NH2 1BV	3	18/11/1991	No

3. **Sort** the database into ascending order of date of birth
4. **Print** one copy of your table in Datasheet View – ensure you put your name in the footer of your printout.

DON'T FORGET

When you are asked to 'sort by name' always sort by surname.

DON'T FORGET

To unsort click on

Remove Sort

DON'T FORGET

Formatting a field as Yes/No will provide a tick box which you can click on

to tick or leave blank as appropriate.

DON'T FORGET

Data in fields formatted for number, currency or date will be right aligned in the column – data in text fields is left aligned.

FORMS

TO CREATE A FORM

It is often easier to input data into a table using a **Form**. When you create a Form you can design it to suit your purposes and so that your database makes sense to you. Forms allow you to see information already in the table and to add new information.

Using the **Form Wizard** is the most straightforward method of creating a Form.

> **DON'T FORGET**
>
> You **MUST** set up all the fields in the table **before** creating a Form and make sure the Table is closed while making changes through the Form.

The Form Wizard provides a number of steps which will enable you to select the source for your Form as well as the fields you want to include, the layout and the title.

 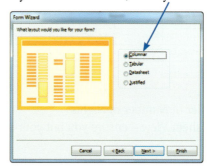 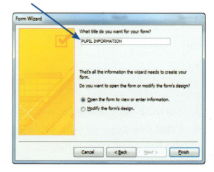

When you have worked through the Wizard your completed form should look like this:

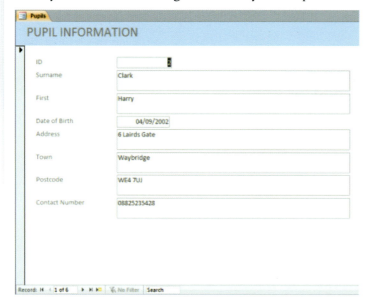

> **DON'T FORGET**
>
> Make sure you know the difference between *Page* Header/Footer and *Form* Header/Footer. *Page* Header/Footer will appear at the top/bottom of **every** page. The *Form* Header will be at the start of the Form while the Form Footer will appear immediately after the Form finishes – this could be half-way down the page!

Add a new record by clicking on New (blank) record button:

If you want to make any changes to your Form, for example, add your name to the footer, then click on View and switch to Design View.

In Design View, the Form Header and Form Footer are automatically shown. Right click with your mouse in Form Header area to show Page Header/Footer.

 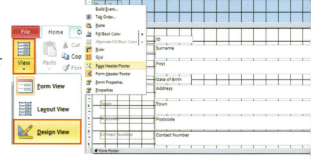

THINGS TO DO AND THINK ABOUT

Now try some of these exercises which will test your knowledge of setting up a database form: entering, editing and deleting data using the form and printing. *These exercises are based on the tables you created in the previous tasks.*

TASK 1

1. Open the database file **Pupil Information** and create a form based on the **Pupils** table. Use the Wizard and include all the fields and use the title **PUPIL INFORMATION**.
2. Use the form to add the following records to the table:

Surname	First Name	Date of Birth	Address	Town	Postcode	Contact Number
Kane	Ewan	03/08/03	73 South Street	Bridgeton	BN2 8JH	01765383920
Hann	George	23/05/03	42 The Grange	Waybridge	WE6 2TD	05542526754
Schmidt	Yosef	17/12/02	16 Farm Lane	Bridgeton	BN2 9KL	07785651248
Marta	Johnston	04/06/02	23 Lake Road	Bridgeton	BN2 7Hk	07788587418

3. Harry Clark has now enrolled in another school. Delete his record through form view – select his record and go to the Home tab and Records and click on

4. Joanne Smith's address should be 24 Wood Road – please update her record
5. In Design View add your name to the page footer
6. Print the record for Ewan Kane in form view

 DON'T FORGET

When adding your name to the form you **MUST** use the Label button to create a text box.

 DON'T FORGET

Once you delete the record you cannot undo, so ensure you are deleting the correct one!

 DON'T FORGET

To print only one record in form view, display that record on your screen. Go to File then Print and in the Print dialogue box click on Selected Record(s) then click OK.

TASK 2

1. Open the data file **Holiday Bookings** and create a form based on the **Holidays** table. Use the Wizard and include all the fields and use the title **HOLIDAY BOOKINGS**
2. Use the form to add the following records to the table:

Title	First Name	Surname	Holiday Destination	Cost of Holiday	Deposit Paid	Date of Departure	No of Nights
Miss	Barbara	Jordan	Minorca	£680	Yes	02/08/2015	10
Mr	James	Ramsay	Crete	£350	No	17/07/2015	7
Mrs	Meg	Richards	Corfu	£380	No	25/07/2015	7

3. Joe Wilson has decided he no longer wishes to go to Ibiza so delete this record
4. There has been an error in Joan Green's booking – amend her record to show she is going to Minorca not Majorca.
5. In design view add your name to the page footer
6. Print the record for Meg Richards in form view

 DON'T FORGET

Can't see any of the tables, queries, forms or reports you have created? Ensure you select All Access Objects in the Navigation Pane at the left-hand side of your screen.

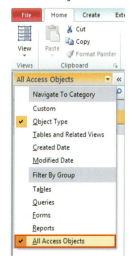

TASK 3

1. Open the database file **Students** and create a form based on the **Student Information** table. Include all the fields and use the title **STUDENTS**.
2. Use the form to add the following records to the table:

First Name	Surname	Street	Town	Postcode	Year Group	Date of Birth	Leaver
Jordan	Scott	23 River View	Newtown	NW7 4TU	1	06/06/1993	No
Claire	Deacon	10 Lamb Street	Newtown	NW4 8UJ	3	07/08/1992	No
Blair	Anderson	32 Chestnut Grove	Northwich	NW2 7KL	4	12/11/1991	Yes

3. In design view add your name to the form footer
4. Print the record for Claire Deacon in form view

SORTING ON TWO FIELDS AND QUERIES

SORTING ON TWO FIELDS

Sorting on one field is very straightforward – sorting on two fields is a little trickier! Very often you want to sort one field then apply a further sort on another field; for example, you want to sort your database containing pupils' information firstly by Town and then within Town you want to sort by Surname. To specify which field to sort on first go to the Home tab, click on Advanced then select Advanced Filter Sort.

A grid will open. Double click on the field name of the first field to be sorted then double click on the name of the second field. Select either Ascending or Descending Sort for each field then click on Toggle Filter to apply the sort criteria.

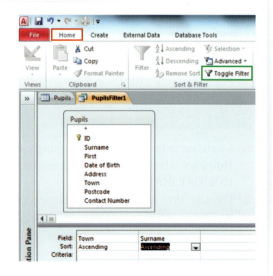

DON'T FORGET

Access sorts on fields from left to right – you must ensure they have been entered into the grid in the correct sort order

DON'T FORGET

Both tables and queries can be sorted in this way.

DON'T FORGET

Wrong fields? Wrong sort order? Click on Clear Grid to start again:

ONLINE

For some great practical tasks on sorting on two fields, head to www.brightredbooks.net/N5AdminIT

QUERIES

To create a Query

A query lets you **search** for specific information in a table – it is like asking a question. The results of the Query can be sorted and printed in the same way as when you are dealing with tables. Queries can be saved for future use or if you want to edit them.

For example, in the database **Holidays** you want to find all those who are going to Corfu. You will find this information in the field called Holiday Destination.

In the Create tab select Query Design

The Show Table dialogue box will open. Select the table you want to run your search on and click on Add

Add the fields you require to the search grid by double clicking on each field name.

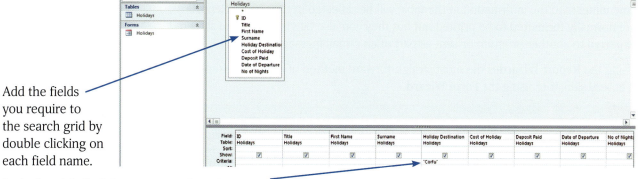

In the line labelled Criteria enter the information you are looking for – in this example enter Corfu under the Holiday Destination field. To see which records match this criteria, click on ! at the start of the ribbon.

The results of the search are:

The format of the field will dictate how you structure your criteria. The above example uses a text field so in this case just key in an exact match of the word

ID ▾	Title ▾	First Name ▾	Surname ▾	Holiday Destination ▾	Cost of Holiday ▾	Deposit Paid ▾	Date of Departure ▾	No of Nights ▾
1	Mr	John	Fallon	Corfu	£500	☑	26/04/2015	7
9	Mrs	Meg	Richards	Corfu	£380	☐	25/07/2015	7
✱ (New)						☐		

(or words) you are looking for under the appropriate field. To find either an exact match or a matching range in fields formatted for number, currency or date, use mathematical symbols as shown below.

FORMAT OF FIELD	CRITERIA	WHAT IS USED IN THE SEARCH
Text	Exact match of word	text
Number or Currency	Greater than Greater than or equal to Less than Less than or equal to	> >= < <= NOTE: Do **NOT** include £ sign when looking for currency amounts
Dates	Before After Between dates – use the phrase 'between (date) and (date)'	< > e.g. Between 1 1 14 and 31 3 14
Yes/No ☑ ☐	Yes No	Yes No

DON'T FORGET

Search not working? Check your spelling matches the word you are looking for and check you are using the right field.

DON'T FORGET

Want to specify criteria but don't want to see the field? Remove the tick from Show line.

REPORTS

TO CREATE A REPORT

A database report allows you to summarise and print information from a database table simply and efficiently. Reports are often based on a query and can be formatted to present the information in the most readable way. Reports can be run at any time and will always reflect the current data from the database – additions, deletions or amendments to the information in the table will be reflected in the report. Reports are normally formatted to be printed out but they can also be viewed on the screen, exported to another program or sent as part of an e-mail message.

Using the **Report Wizard** is the most straightforward method of creating a Report. It is very similar to using the **Form Wizard.**

The first window will enable you to select the source for your Report as well as the fields you want to include, then click Next. The second window allows you to specify any groupings within your data, but ignore this window and just click on Next.

The next window lets you sort a particular field(s), but it is often better to sort the table or query **BEFORE** you start to create the report

The next step is to decide on layout. Tabular is the one that is most often used **BUT think carefully whether you want Portrait or Landscape layout** – if you are including a lot of fields or fields that have a lot of information in them, then choose landscape.

The final step is to give your report a suitable title – anyone picking up a copy of the report should know exactly what the information is telling them.

When you click on Finish, the report is created and it is shown in Print Preview. Check all data is visible.

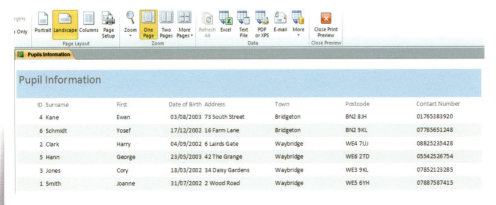

ID	Surname	First	Date of Birth	Address	Town	Postcode	Contact Number
4	Kane	Ewan	03/08/2003	73 South Street	Bridgeton	BN2 8JH	01765383920
6	Schmidt	Yosef	17/12/2002	16 Farm Lane	Bridgeton	BN2 9KL	07785651248
2	Clark	Harry	04/09/2002	6 Lairds Gate	Waybridge	WE4 7UJ	08825235428
5	Hann	George	23/05/2003	42 The Grange	Waybridge	WE6 2TD	05542526754
3	Jones	Cory	18/03/2002	34 Daisy Gardens	Waybridge	WE3 9KL	07852123285
1	Smith	Joanne	31/07/2002	2 Wood Road	Waybridge	WE5 6YH	07887587415

DON'T FORGET

You **MUST** set up the table or query **before** creating a report and carry out any sorting instructions. Save the table or query then close before starting your report.

THINGS TO DO AND THINK ABOUT

Now try some of these exercises which will test your knowledge of querying, sorting a database table on two fields and printing. *These exercises are based on the tables you created in the previous tasks.*

TASK 1

Open the **Pupil Information** database. Sort the table **Pupils** into ascending order of town and descending order of surname. Publish the table to Word, put your name in the footer and print one copy.

TASK 2

Use the database **Pupil Information** and the table **Pupils.** Include all fields in your query design and search for

(a) Pupils who live in Bridgeton

(b) Pupils born after 1 May 2003. Hint: use >1 5 03 in your criteria

(c) Pupils born in 2002. Hint: always include day, month and year when searching for dates. Here you are looking for dates between 1 1 02 and 31 12 02

TASK 3

Open the database file **Pupil Information** and using the **Pupils** table create a report showing first name, surname and contact telephone number of all pupils in alphabetical order. Use the title **PUPIL TELEPHONE NUMBERS**. Put your name in the page footer and print one copy.

TASK 4

Using the **Pupils** database table find those pupils who live in Waybridge. Create a report showing their first name, surname and date of birth sorted in descending order of date of birth. Use the title **WAYBRIDGE PUPILS**. Put your name in the report footer and print one copy.

DON'T FORGET

Close Print Preview and make any changes to the layout of the report in Design View. Remember when adding your name to the header/footer you MUST use the label button: *Aa*

View

DON'T FORGET

When you key in your criteria let the computer add any relevant syntax, for example, dates make use of #

DON'T FORGET

The Page Footer automatically contains the date the report was created and page number/ number of pages. These can be deleted if not required.

DON'T FORGET

Make sure you know the difference between Page Header/Footer and Report Header/Footer.

ONLINE

For more great practical tasks, head to www.brightredbooks. net/N5AdminIT

WORD PROCESSING

SETTING UP A WORD DOCUMENT 1

To ensure you are able to present documents professionally with a variety of fonts, formats and layouts, you must be familiar with the Ribbon in Word. The Ribbon is split into a number of tabs and within each of the tabs you will find groups of buttons or commands and menus which will allow you to carry out a number of actions.

DON'T FORGET

More options are available within certain groups of commands when you see ⌐ at the bottom right-hand corner. When you click any of these arrows, dialogue boxes will open giving you more options. This icon is known as the **Dialogue Box Launcher**.

WORD TABS

Home tab

The *Home* tab allows you to **select** and **change font, font size** and **style** including **bold, italics** and **underline** as well as **shading** and **aligning text** and to change **line spacing** and use **bullets** and **numbering**.

Insert tab

The *Insert* tab allows you to insert **new page; tables; pictures, graphics** and **shapes; headers and footers** and **page numbers; text boxes; date and time** and **symbols**.

Page Layout tab

With the *Page Layout* tab you can **set** and **change margins**, change the **orientation** of your document from portrait to landscape and insert **Page Borders**.

Quick Access Toolbar

In addition to the tabs described above, the Quick Access Toolbar is available at the top left-hand corner of your screen. This can be customised to include commands that you use very frequently, for example, Quick Print or Undo, and so will save you time searching for these commands.

DON'T FORGET

Always work with your ruler visible on your screen as this helps when you are laying out your page. Go to View tab and select ☑ Ruler

SETTING UP A WORD DOCUMENT: AN OVERVIEW

When setting up any Word document you must think about:

- margins
- font and font size
- format of text
- line spacing
- aligning text
- headers and footers

Let's have a closer look at each of these now.

MARGINS (PAGE LAYOUT TAB)

Margins are the areas around the document that do not contain any text or graphics. Most documents that you will work with will use margins of 2.5 cm. Any changes to the margins can be made using the Page Layout tab, Margins then Custom Margins.

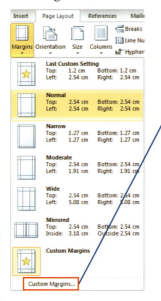

A4 document – Portrait layout

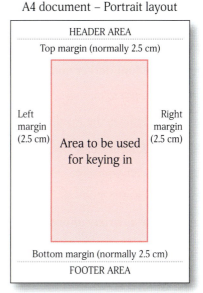

FONT AND FONT SIZE (HOME TAB)

There is a large variety of fonts available and the size of the font can be increased or decreased according to how you want the text within your document to be presented, for example:

This is Calibri size 16 point

This is Arial Black size 14 point

THIS IS STENCIL SIZE 10

This is Jokerman size 18

DON'T FORGET

If you are unsure how big or small to make the font select the text with your mouse and use either of these buttons A˙ A˙ to gradually increase or decrease the size of the font.

If you have keyed in text and you wish to change to the case, for example, from lowercase to capital letters, you can use the Change Case button available in the Home tab.

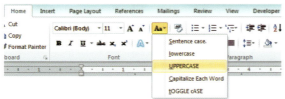

Put these words into caps   would very easily become   PUT THESE WORDS INTO CAPS

 THINGS TO DO AND THINK ABOUT

Try using some of the different fonts and font sizes for different types of documents. What sort of document would a font like

Jokerman size 18

be appropriate for?

SETTING UP A WORD DOCUMENT 2

FORMAT OF TEXT (HOME TAB)

As well as choosing a font and the size of the font, it is possible to change the **format** of the text. The formats that are available are:

Bold – makes the font darker and thicker

Italics – the font slopes to the side

<u>Underscore – underlines the word(s)</u>

<u>***Or a combination of all three***</u>

~~Score through is also available~~

as is either _{subscript} or ^{superscript}

or you can choose a variety of text effects such as shadow, glow or reflection.

DON'T FORGET

More options are available by clicking here:

LINE SPACING (HOME TAB)

This is the amount of space between lines of text. Examples of some of the most commonly used line spacing are:

DON'T FORGET

Word defaults to give additional space before and after lines of text that you might not want. In the Paragraph dialogue box change Spacing Before and After to 0 and Line spacing to Single.

Single line spacing

> This is an example of **1.0 (single) line spacing**. There is no space left between the lines.

Line and a half

> This is an example of
> **1.5 line spacing**.
> The lines of text are spaced out a little.

Double line spacing

> This is an example of
>
> **2.0 (double) line spacing**.
>
> Here a 'blank' line is left between each line of text.

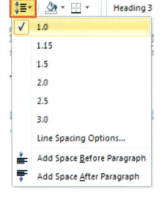

To change the default click Set As Default, then click All documents based on the Normal template. All your documents should now open up with these settings.

ALIGNING TEXT (HOME TAB)

Text can be aligned relative to the left margin. Examples are:

> This is an example of text that is **left** aligned.

> This is an example of text that is **centred** across the page.

> This is an example of text that is **right** aligned.

> This is an example of text that is **justified**. Text in books is often aligned like this.

HEADERS AND FOOTERS (INSERT TAB)

These are inserted either within the top margin or the bottom margin of the document and usually provide information such as page numbers, date, file name or author name. Any text that is inserted in either the header or the footer will appear on all pages of your document. There are a variety of layouts to choose from.

When inserting page numbers in either the header or footer, it is easier to put your cursor where you want the page number to appear then, under Header & Footer Tools, select Current Position and then Plain Number.

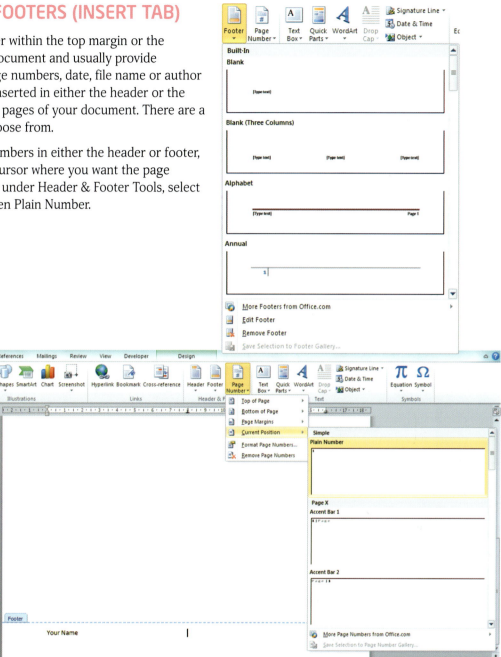

THINGS TO DO AND THINK ABOUT

The Show/Hide button ¶, available in the Home tab, can be used to show exactly where you have used the space bar, the return key or the tab key within the document. This helps when you want to delete additional blank pages that may appear at the end of your document!

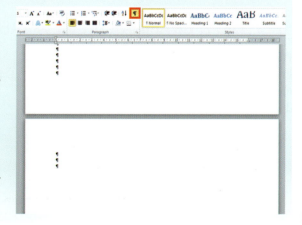

The return key has been used a number of times here and so these 'codes' can be deleted to remove this blank page

REVIEW TAB

COMMENTS

Comments can be added to a Word document to give further information or to give instructions to the operator. They are shown at the right-hand side of the document.

Once the instruction has been read and carried out, the comment can be deleted by clicking on it then selecting Delete in the Review tab.

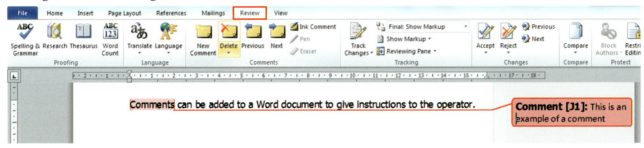

Printing a document without the comments showing

If the comments are not deleted and you do not want to print them go to the File tab, Print then Settings. Use the menu at Print All Pages and ensure Print Markup has not been selected by **removing** the tick.

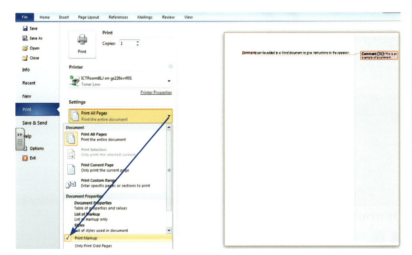

SPELLING & GRAMMAR (REVIEW TAB)

While Word often picks up spelling and grammatical errors as you key in, it is always best to do a final check of your document before you print.

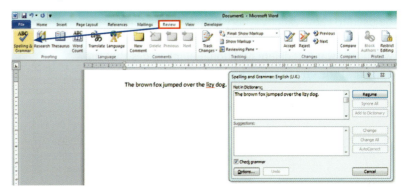

MANUSCRIPT CORRECTIONS

Often the author of a document would like changes to be made either to the format of the text or to the words themselves. Symbols are used to indicate what the changes should be. These symbols are most often written in the left margin along with any specific instruction and the word to be changed within the text is underlined or highlighted in some way.

DON'T FORGET

The underline is only to highlight which word in the paragraph needs to be edited – do not underline the word unless the u/score instruction is given!

Symbol found in the margin	Example of edit required	What is means	Corrected text
lc	Check your document <u>C</u>arefully for errors.	**Lower case** – change the capital letter to a small letter	Check your document carefully for errors.
uc	The name of the little boy is <u>j</u>ohn.	**Upper case** – change the small letter to a capital letter	The name of the little boy is John.
caps	You must <u>stop</u> at a red light.	**Capital letters** – change the whole word to capitals	You must STOP at a red light.
run on	Our sales have increased.⌐ └This trend is expected to continue.	**Run on** – join 2 paragraphs together and do **not** take a new paragraph	Our sales have increased. This trend is expected to continue.
NP	This is good news for this year.⌐During the course of next year we expect to see	**New paragraph** – take a new paragraph at the point indicated	This is good news for this year. During the course of next year we expect to see ....
Trs	This year ⌐to⌐ compared last year.	**Transpose**	This year compared to last year.
⌐	Tomorrow is another ~~new~~ day.	**Delete** – leave out the word crossed out	Tomorrow is another day.
Stet	~~grey~~ The s<u>k</u>y is blue.	**Stet (let it stand)** – key in the word with the dots underneath	The sky is blue.
and⌃	Bees are black⌃ yellow.	**Insert** – include the word shown	Bees are black and yellow.
⌣	The grass is◯green.	**Close up** – take away the extra space between the words	The grass is green.
#⌃	Zebras are black⌃and white.	Insert space	Zebras are black and white.
u/score	Do this <u>immediately</u>.	**Underscore** – underline the word	Do this <u>immediately</u>.
bold	Do <u>not</u> enter.	**Embolden** – use bold	Do **not** enter.

THINGS TO DO AND THINK ABOUT

Try this exercise to test your knowledge of manuscript corrections.

Instructions:

1. Set left and right margins to 2.5 cm and use single line spacing unless otherwise instructed
2. Key in the text and follow all editing instructions
3. When you have completed the task use your spellcheck and proof-read for any errors
4. Put your name in the document footer then save and print

ONLINE

Find some great tasks on word processing at www.brightredbooks.net/N5AdminIT

⌃awful	The flooding caused such⌃destruction.
Stet	The wind was ~~blowing~~ <u>howling</u> through the trees.
trs	Lucky is the name of the ⌐black⌐little⌐cat.
caps	You must <u>stop</u> at a red light.
⌐	He ~~was~~ is afraid of the dark.
lc	When the sun <u>S</u>hone he felt happy.

Use double line spacing for this task

BULLETS AND NUMBERING

USING BULLETS AND NUMBERING

Bullet points and numbering are used to create lists and can also be useful in organising and adding emphasis to headings and paragraphs. Arranging text in a list can make it easier to read and is more visually attractive. Often the language used within bullet points is abbreviated.

DON'T FORGET

All bulleted and numbered lists in particular should be created automatically within Word – it is then easy to insert or delete an item and the list will automatically update and renumber the previous items.

EXAMPLE

Fruit

◆ Apples
◆ Oranges
◆ Bananas

Bullets and numbering commands are found in the Home tab and menus give you more options.

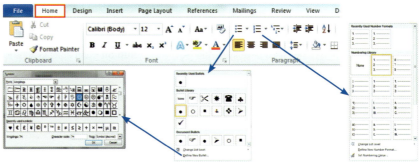

Want to change how your bullet point looks? Click on Define New Bullet and you can select your own symbols for the bullet points – have a look through all the available Fonts and then try it for yourself!

 THINGS TO DO AND THINK ABOUT

Now try some of these exercises which will test your knowledge of bullets and numbering as well as your skills in changing fonts, line spacing, text formatting and layout.

Instructions:

1. Set left and right margins to 2.5 cm and use single line spacing unless otherwise instructed
2. Key in the text and follow all editing instructions
3. When you have completed the task use your spellcheck and proof-read for any errors
4. Put your name in the footer of the document then save and print each task

 TASK 1

caps
and
bold

Countries of the World

• France
• Spain
• Portugal
• United States of America

Use double line spacing and bullet points as shown

 TASK 2

bold

TRAINING PROGRAMME – ADMINISTRATIVE SERVICES DEPARTMENT

Course   u/score

Your course will include:

1. Word Processing
2. Spreadsheets
3. Databases
4. Electronic Mail
5. Internet

number the display sections at the left margin

All members of staff should inform their line manager what area of the course is their main priority.

⊙ TASK 3

caps <u>Open Day</u>　　　　　　**Use a font of your choice for this exercise**

Come along and join in! Attractions include:

- Guided walks
- Falconry exhibitions
- Pageants
- Craft stalls

bullet this list at the left margin and use 1.5 line spacing

⊙ TASK 4

Bold <u>Health and safety</u>

Workers are protected by:

<u>The Health and Safety at Work Act 1974</u>　　**Use larger font size**

Employers have a duty to provide a safe workplace for employees.

The following steps should be taken to prevent accidents:

- ◆ keep the fire exits clear
- ◆ do not leave fire doors ajar
- ◆ keep floors and stairways in good repair
- ◆ close filing cabinets when not in use
- ◆ switch off electrical appliances

Use bullet points of your choice for the display section and indent to 2 cm

Please ensure that any breach of the above rules is reported to the Safety Officer.

DON'T FORGET

To move (or **indent**) the bullet point or number a certain distance from the margin, open the Paragraph dialogue box and change the Left Indentation. Try this in the next task.

⊙ TASK 5

Bold and caps

<u>Customer service</u>

Number these items at the margin and use double line spacing for this section

Good customer service means:

1. Happy customers who will keep coming back to the organisation
2. Happy staff who will stay with the organisation and do a good job
3. A good reputation for the organisation which will attract new customers
4. Increased sales and higher profits

⊙ TASK 6

Bold **Skills and Qualities of an Administrative Assistant**

＾ **able**

A skill is something you are ＾ to do. The skills of an Administrative Assistant include:

- ICT skills
- communication skills
- problem-solving skills
- teamwork skills

Use 2 different types of bullets

A quality describes what kind of person you are. The qualities of an Administrative Assistant include:

- ♦ organised
- ♦ keen to learn
- ♦ polite
- ♦ helpful and friendly

TABLES

INSERTING A TABLE

Aligning text in columns in a Word document can be time consuming if you try to do it using tabs and spaces. However **inserting a table** will allow you to align columns and rows of text with ease and will give you options with regards to borders, shading and other formatting; you can even sort and carry out simple calculations on any columns that contain numbers. *Tables are a very good method for creating* **Forms**, *for example, customer feedback surveys, booking forms, etc.*

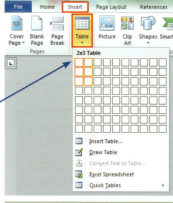

There are many ways to insert a table. The quickest way to create a table from scratch is to go to the **Insert** tab then click on the **Table** button when your cursor is positioned at the place in your document where you would like the table to begin. A grid will pop up allowing you to select how many rows and columns you would like your table to contain. Use your mouse to select the number of rows and columns by highlighting the boxes (text at the top left of the grid will indicate what your selection is). When you have specified the correct number of rows and columns, click once, and your table will be created.

The table created will have uniform columns and rows but you can customise your table by right-clicking on the table handle (the double-headed arrow at the top left corner of the table) and use the options on the shortcut menu to make changes.

For example, to change the width of the columns to fit the contents as shown below, use AutoFit to Contents:

Class	Level	Room No
Introduction to IT	Beginner	1A
Complex WP Exercises	Advanced	16F

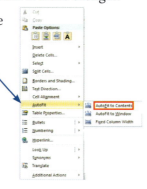

JUST A WEE NOTE

Hint: if you don't immediately see what you need on the shortcut menu, select **Table Properties** for more advanced options.

TABLE TOOLS

When you create a table, additional commands are then available under **Table Tools**.

Design

Here you can add Shading and Borders to cells within the table or the entire table.

Layout

Here you can add or delete columns or rows, change the direction of the text as well as sort the table and carry out calculations.

THINGS TO DO AND THINK ABOUT

Now try some of these exercises which will test your knowledge of inserting tables, adding or deleting rows and columns, borders, shading, sorting data, alignment of text within cells and formulae.

Instructions:

1. Set left and right margins to 2.5 cm and use single line spacing unless instructed otherwise
2. Key in the text and follow all editing instructions
3. When you have completed the task use your spellcheck and proof-read for any errors
4. Put your name in the header of the document then save and print each task

 TASK 1

Sort the table by STOCK CODE

ITEM	STOCK CODE	COLOUR	PRICE
Pencils	PY/34	HB	£5.50
Pens	PN/67	blue	£1.20
Rulers	RL/11	clear	£2.25
Ring binders	RB/95	marine blue	£0.65

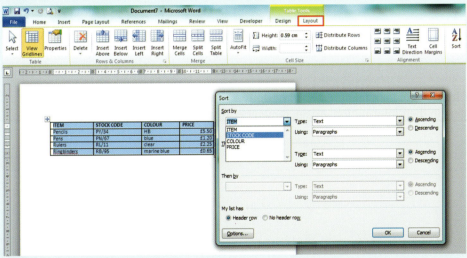

 TASK 2

Shade the top row – adjust the columns to AutoFit to Contents.

First Name	Last Name	Marks
Jill	Smith	50
Eve	Jacks	94
John	Dorris	80
Adam	Johnston	67

 TASK 3

Sort in ascending order of Total Goals

Team	Goals Last Season	Goals This Season	Total Goals
Swallow Boys Club	24	7	31
Midweek Juniors	17	5	22
Eagle Rovers	17	2	19
Allerdyce Athletics	15	2	17

Tables are made up of rows and columns and cells, so when you choose formatting options think whether you want to include the whole table or just the cells you have selected with your mouse.

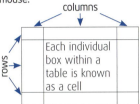

Not enough rows in the table you have created? Go to the last cell at the right-hand side of the last row and press the tab key – ⬚ – a blank row will now be added to your table!

To sort: select the whole table then under Table Tools and Layout click on ⬚. The Sort dialogue box will open giving you choices as to which column or columns you want sorted and whether ascending or descending.

Use your mouse to select only the top row of your table. Shading is available under Table Tools, then Design. If you select a very dark colour the font colour will automatically change to white!

To remove the gridlines: select the table then under Table Tools, Design then Borders; click on No Border.

FORMS

Forms are designed in such a way as to obtain specific information from a large number of people. For example, application forms gather information about candidates for a job – their qualifications and work history – and customer feedback forms find out how customers view the service they have received and give them the opportunity to make suggestions for improvement. Forms can either be printed to allow people to write the information on or they can be set up for completion online.

CREATING A FORM

When you are creating a form, think about **Inserting a Table** then merge cells, expand rows and/or columns as appropriate and make use of borders and shading.

EXAMPLE

Customer First Name		Customer Second Name	
Address			
Telephone Number			

DON'T FORGET

Allow space for people to fill in the form and extend the boxes by dragging the lines rather than entering spaces or pressing the return key.

Alternatively...

Rather than using a table, your form might contain either solid or dotted lines for people to use when they are filling in their information. Again, remember to allow plenty of space here!

EXAMPLE

Name: . . . .

>2LS

Address: . . . .

To set up **leader dots** like this, go to the Home tab, open the Paragraph dialogue box and select Tabs. Set a **Right** tab at the right margin (16 cm) then choose either Leader dots or a solid line. You must click on **Set** then **OK**.

Key in the text, for example, Name: and now press the Tab key on your keyboard:

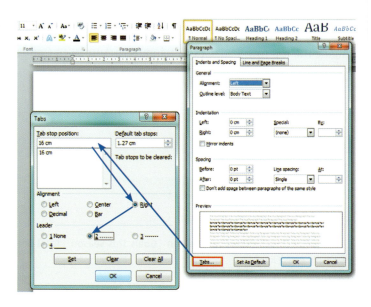

THINGS TO DO AND THINK ABOUT

Now try some of these exercises which will test your knowledge of leader dots, inserting tables, adding or deleting rows and columns, borders, shading, merging cells and alignment of text within cells.

Instructions:

1. Set left and right margins to 2.5 cm
2. Create the forms shown – for some of the tasks hints have been given
3. When you have completed the task use your spellcheck and proof-read for any errors
4. Put your name in the footer of the document then save and print each task

 TASK 1

Insert a relevant graphic at the top right-hand side of the page

IT-TRAIN LIMITED

APPLICATION FOR ICT TRAINING

Name of Course:	
Course Code:	
Date of Course:	
Location of Course:	
Name of Applicant(s):	
Cost per Applicant:	
Total Cost Payable:	

Payment is due when course availability is confirmed.

 TASK 2

MEETING ROOM BOOKING FORM

Name: ....

Department: ....

Date required: ....

Time required: ....

Catering requirements:
Coffee/Tea ☐   Buffet Lunch ☐

Equipment required:
Flip Chart ☐   Digital Projector ☐

ONLINE

For more great tasks to practice, head to www.brightredbooks.net/N5AdminIT

JUST A WEE NOTE

Hint: Go to Insert tab and Symbol menu; then More symbols; and find a suitable symbol for the tick box.

BUSINESS DOCUMENTS: MEMORANDUM

BUSINESS DOCUMENTS: AN OVERVIEW

A variety of documents are used by businesses to communicate with both staff and customers. Organisations often follow their own **house style** to ensure consistency of presentation or they make use of **document templates** which are stored centrally and available to all employees. Using a template saves time and ensures everyone is using the same layout.

MEMORANDUM

This is a note that is sent **between employees of the same organisation**. Memos should be brief and to the point and are often used to instruct or remind employees or highlight events that are happening within the organisation.

DON'T FORGET

Memorandum is sometimes just called memo.

EXAMPLE

MEMORANDUM

>3LS

To: John Flynn, Regional Manager

>2LS

From: Mike Smith, Sales Director

>2LS

Date: 26 January 2014

>2LS

Subject: Sales Conference

>3LS

I am writing to remind you that the next Sales Review Conference will take place on the first Thursday of next month in the Conference Suite on level 5.

At the meeting I would like you to present the sales figures for your area to date by way of a short PowerPoint presentation. As there will be a number of presentations that day, can you please ensure that your talk lasts no more than 5 minutes.

The name and job title of the person **receiving** the message

The name and job title of the person **sending** the message

The date the message is being sent

The topic of the message

The message should be keyed in starting from the left margin, in single line spacing and with 2 returns between each paragraph unless otherwise instructed

DON'T FORGET

>2LS or 3LS is an indication of how many times you should press the return key.

THINGS TO DO AND THINK ABOUT

Now try some of these exercises which will test your knowledge of the layout of a Memo as well as bullets and numbering and inserting a table.

Instructions:

1. Set left and right margins to 2.5 cm
2. Use the layout given on the previous page
3. Key in the text and follow all editing instructions
4. When you have completed the task use your spellcheck and proof-read for any errors
5. Put your name in the footer of the document then save and print each task

TASK 1

MEMORANDUM

TO:	Joanne Waters, Head of Sales
FROM:	Marcia Grant, IT Services
DATE:	(today's date)
SUBJECT:	File Management and Housekeeping

Can you remind staff that it is important that any document they create is given an appropriate file name and that it is stored in the correct folder within their own 'My Documents' area. Any unwanted files should be deleted and the recycle bin should be emptied. All files are backed-up centrally on a daily basis so there should not be any problems if a file is accidently deleted.

If there are any new members of staff in your department who feel that they would like training on any aspect of the system, can you please have them contact me.

 TASK 2

MEMORANDUM

TO:	Mike Jones
FROM:	Keith Struthers
DATE:	(today's date)
SUBJECT:	Safety Issues

Following the recent health and safety inspection, the following actions have now been taken:

1. The faulty bulb in the Emergency Exit sign has been replaced.
2. Electronic magnets have now been added to the corridor fire doors, which means they will close automatically when the fire bell is activated.
3. The fire extinguisher in the staff rest room has now been repaired and staff have been instructed not to tamper with it.

Our premises will be inspected by the Fire Service next Friday (14th February).

 TASK 3

MEMORANDUM

TO:	All Team Leaders
FROM:	Stacey Brown, Staff Development Officer
DATE:	(today's date)
SUBJECT:	Training Courses

There are a number of places available on the next Management Development Programme that is due to start at the beginning of next month. Any member of your team who is interested in further progression within the company is eligible to be considered providing they meet the following criteria:

1. the employee has 3 years' service with the company
2. the employee has an degree qualification or equivalent

Interested members of staff should complete form MDPAPP and submit it to me by the end of next week.

 ONLINE

For more great tasks to practice, head to www.brightredbooks.net/N5AdminIT

BUSINESS DOCUMENTS: BUSINESS LETTERS

WHAT IS A BUSINESS LETTER?

A business letter is a document written in formal language, usually used when an organisation is writing to customers, suppliers or another organisation.

EXAMPLE

Here is an example of the layout of a business letter.

OFFICE ESSENTIALS
New Business Park
ANTOWN
AY43 4UN

Tel: 01764 789325
E-mail: enquiries@offess.co.uk

>3LS

JB/Your initials

Reference – the initials of the person signing the letter then your initials

>2LS

Today's Date

Today's date – e.g. 21 February 2014

>2LS

Mr J L Smith
27 Wells Drive
ANYTOWN
AY45 8BN

Inside address – the name of the person **receiving** the letter. Note the name and each part of the address are on separate lines.

>2LS

Dear Mr Smith

Salutation – the name of the person **receiving** the letter. Sometimes the letter is addressed Dear Sir or Dear Madam

>2LS

OFFICE EQUIPMENT

Subject Heading – the topic of the letter

>2LS

Thank you for your enquiry about our new range of office equipment. We are pleased to enclose our brochure, and note below some of our special offers.

>3LS

2-drawer filing cabinet	£49.90
Workstation desk	£89.99
Adjustable swivel chair	£34.50

>3LS

All of the above prices exclude VAT, and represent a saving of 25% on our normal prices.

If you require any more information, please telephone us on the above number. We look forward to receiving your first order.

Yours sincerely

Complimentary close – if you know the name of the person then it's Yours sincerely. If the letter is addressed Dear Sir or Dear Madam then it's Yours faithfully

>6LS

Joan Black
Sales Director

The name and job title of the person **sending** the letter

>3LS

Enc

Any enclosures with the letter are indicated here – e.g. a brochure or price list etc

THINGS TO DO AND THINK ABOUT

Now try some of these exercises which will test your knowledge of the layout of a business letter as well as editor's corrections and inserting a table.

Instructions:

1. Set left and right margins to 2.5 cm and the top margin to 4 cm
2. Use the layout given on the previous page – always insert an appropriate reference and make sure you complete the complimentary close with either Yours sincerely or Yours faithfully
3. Key in the text and follow all editing instructions
4. When you have completed the task use your spellcheck and proof-read for any errors
5. Put your name in the header of the document and save and print each task

TASK 1

Ref

Today's date

Mr Steven Bell
12 Acacia Drive
BRIDGETOWN
BD56 8UH

Dear Mr Bell

INVITATION TO ATTEND FOR INTERVIEW

I am writing to confirm that we would like you to attend an interview on
Monday 6 June at 10.00 am.   **Bold**

As you will have the opportunity to tour our manufacturing facility at this
location and meet with our production team it is likely that you will be with us
until approximately 4.00 pm. Lunch will be provided around 1.00 pm and light
refreshments will be available throughout the day.

Please phone me on the above telephone number, extension 323, to confirm your
attendance.

Yours etc.

John Simpson
Production Director

 TASK 2

Ref

Today's date

The Manager
Royal Hotel
123 High Street
Buckton
LH21 4KJ
Dear Sir

BOOKING CONFIRMATION

I write to confirm the following accommodation and equipment requirements for our
Sales Team meeting that is taking place on Tuesday 19 April.

Time	Room	Number of People	Requirements
9.30 am – 11.30 am	Lake Room	14	TV, video
12.15 pm – 3.30 pm	Tudor Suite	25	Data projector, AV Screen

In addition to the above we will require tea/coffee and biscuits at 10.00 am, lunch at
1.15 pm and light refreshments at 3.15 pm for all participants.

Please contact me if you have any questions regarding the above.

Yours faithfully

Christine Clarke
Senior Administrator

 ONLINE

Head to www.brightredbooks.
net/N5AdminIT for another
business letter task.

 DON'T FORGET

Use a table for the display but
remove the gridlines before
printing.

BUSINESS DOCUMENTS: AGENDAS AND ITINERARIES
NOTICE OF MEETING AND AGENDA

Notice of meeting and agenda is the document that give those attending meetings prior notice of what is being discussed. A Notice of meeting and agenda also gives all the relevant details of who is meeting and when and where the meeting will take place.

EXAMPLE

Here is an example of the layout of a Notice of meeting and agenda:

CARRON SPORTS COMMITTEE   Make use of bold to highlight headings

>3LS

A meeting of the Carron Sports Committee will be held in the Main Conference Room on Monday 18 April 2015 at 2030 hours.

>3LS

AGENDA   Always include the type of meeting, the venue, the date and the time

>2LS

1. Apologies
2. Minutes of the last meeting
3. Matters arising
4. Treasurer's report ◄
5. Golf outing ◄
6. Cross country race ◄
7. Any other business
8. Date of next meeting

These items may vary. Items highlighted in yellow are standard items that appear on most Agendas

DON'T FORGET

Use automatic numbering for each item so that the list can be updated easily.

TASK

Complete the next task following the instructions provided on p 64.

Solapanel sales

Notice of meeting   caps

The monthly Branch Managers' meeting will be held in Conference Room 1, on Friday 22 March 20__ at 1000 hours.

AGENDA

1. (Minutes of previous meeting)   trs
2. (Apologies for absence)
3. Business arising from the minutes
4. Monthly targets
5. Performance-related pay
6. Training arrangements
7. Branch ~~re-organising~~ ∧ **restructuring**
8. Any other businesses
9. Date of next meeting

ITINERARIES

An **itinerary** is a detailed plan listing hour by hour what a person is scheduled to do, where, and with whom. **All times are expressed in 24-hour format** and where there may be time differences, local times are shown.

EXAMPLE

Here is an example of the layout of an itinerary:

ITINERARY: Peter Black | Make use of bold to highlight headings
>2LS

Final of 'Young Project Manager of the Year', Liverpool
>2LS

Saturday 15 February – Sunday 16 February 2014
>3LS

Saturday 15 February
>2 LS

1123 hours	Train departs Pitlochry station to Edinburgh Waverley station
1323 hours	Arrive Edinburgh Waverley station
1416 hours	Depart Edinburgh Waverley station to Preston station
1648 hours	Arrive Preston station
1704 hours	Depart Preston station to Liverpool Lime Street station
1801 hours	Arrive Liverpool Lime Street station. Taxi to Thistle Liverpool Hotel, Chapel Street, Liverpool, L3 9RE. Accommodation book reference: 7843983.
1930 hours	Mr Simon Brake, Northern Area Manager, will meet you in hotel reception. A table has been reserved in Café Rendezvous, the hotel restaurant.

>3LS

Sunday 16 February

0900 hours	Taxi to Liverpool Arena
1000–1230 hours	Attend final of 'Young Project Manager of the Year' at the Liverpool Arena. Taxi to Lime Street station.
1322 hours	Train departs Liverpool Lime Street station to York station
1535 hours	Arrive York station
1555 hours	Depart York station to Pitlochry station
2030 hours	Arrive Pitlochry station

  THINGS TO DO AND THINK ABOUT

Complete the next task following the instructions provided on p 64.

 ONLINE

Head to www.brightredbooks.net/N5AdminIT for further tasks.

 TASK

ITINERARY: Mr Peter Jones

Trip to London – Tour of QuikPak Production Facilities and Southdean Chamber of Commerce

Monday 21 June 20__

0530 hours	Taxi from home to Edinburgh airport.
0600 hours	Check in for flight TC679 to London City airport.
0700 hours	Flight departs.
0810 hours	Flight arrives London City airport. You will be met in arrivals hall by a representative from QuikPak and taken directly to their facilities.
1230 hours	Taxi from QuikPak to Southdean Chamber of Commerce.
1300 hours	Lunch with Mr Simon Campbell, Chairman, Louise Fitzpatrick, Marketing Director and Cameron Phipps, Business Development Manager.
1530 hours	Taxi to London City airport.
1600 hours	Check in for flight TC678 to Edinburgh airport.
1705 hours	Flight departs.
1815 hours	Flight arrives Edinburgh airport. Taxi home.

DON'T FORGET

By moving the Left Indent marker on the ruler you can create a **hanging indent** which automatically aligns the paragraph without having to use the tab key on every line.

DISPLAYS/POSTERS/MENUS/BOOKLETS

By making use of graphics, page borders, WordArt, different fonts, font sizes, formats (bold, underline, italics) and other options available within Word, it is possible to create some very eye-catching posters and displays.

PAGE BORDERS

Page borders can be accessed from the Page Layout tab and there are numerous styles to choose from, including Art.

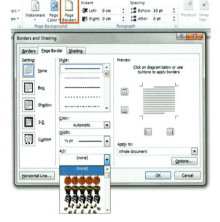

PICTURES

Pictures that have been saved, **Clip Art** and **Shapes** can be inserted using these buttons in the Insert tab.

Picture | Clip Art | Shapes

Always resize using the handles in any of the four corners and drag diagonally. This will ensure your graphic is kept in proportion.

DON'T FORGET

Once the ClipArt image or picture has been inserted into your Word document right click with your mouse, select Wrap Text then Tight. It is then easy to move the graphic around the page to the position you want. You might then decide you want to put it behind text if it interferes with any layouts.

BORDERING TEXT

Text can be bordered by using the Border button in the Home tab. Be careful how much of the text you select with your mouse – if you include the paragraph return then the whole line to the margin will have the border rather than just the word. Use the show/hide button ¶ to reveal where the paragraph returns are.

PRACTICAL EXERCISES

Now try some of these exercises which will test your design skills. Remember, posters should be informative but not over-cluttered!

Instructions:

1. Set left and right margins to 2.5 cm
2. Use the **whole page** and key in the text making use of a variety of fonts and formats – you should use at least two different fonts and two different formats
3. Add appropriate graphics and a page border
4. When you have completed the task, use your spellcheck and proof-read for any errors
5. Put your name in the centre of the footer of the document and save and print each task

TASK 1

Hilltown High School

presents

'Rock 'n' Roll – The Musical'

Wednesday 16 June, Thursday 17 June and Friday 18 June

Doors open 7.00 pm
Performance starts 7.30 pm

Tickets £2.50 available from Music & Drama Department

All monies raised go towards school fund!

TASK 2

House Angels

Lets us take the stress out of housework!

House cleaning, window washing and ironing

Kitchens and bathrooms our speciality

Regular or one-off cleaning

Phone Jenny on 02322 939293 for a
no-obligation quotation

BOOKLETS

Another publication layout you might want to create is a double-sided folded booklet. This is very simple to do using A4 landscape layout and then printing on both sides of the paper.

Half Fold

Start your document by going to the Page Layout tab and open the Page Setup dialogue box. Select Book fold from Multiple pages menu. Click OK and the orientation of the document automatically changes to Landscape.

You will then be able to key in the front page then the inside left, then inside right and finally the back page of the booklet. Remember to print on both sides of the page.

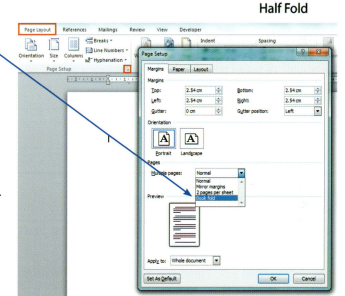

Front Page	Inside Left	Inside Right	Back Page
SUZY'S SNACKS Open daily 8.00 am – 8.00 pm MENU	**Lunch Club** £5.95 all sandwiches, wraps and paninis pre served with skinny fries Tuna melt Sweet Chilli chicken Smoked cheese and ham Cheese and pickle	**Soup & Sandwich Combo** Chef's choice of homemade soup served with a sandwich or toasty with 2 fillings £5.95	**Small Plates** £5.95 all served with vegetables and a choice of potatoes or fries Freshly breaded haddock Whole tail scampi Classic steak pie Chicken tempura Chicken pakora

DON'T FORGET

Go to the Insert tab and Page Break when you want to start a new page.

THINGS TO DO AND THINK ABOUT

Try this booklet for yourself. Centre all text across each page and add a suitable graphic to the front page. Remember to put your name in the footer of the document. Proof-read and use your spellcheck then print on both sides of the paper.

PRACTICE ASSIGNMENT

IT SOLUTIONS FOR ADMINISTRATORS

You are the Administrative Assistant working in the Reservations Department of Elite Travel based in Edinburgh. You are required to carry out a number of tasks for Mrs Erin Jones, Head of Reservations. Here is a summary of the tasks you are required to carry out and the required number of printouts.

TASK NO	TASK	NUMBER OF PRINTOUTS
1	Create letter headed paper to be used by the company	1
2	Create a database of customers using a form	2
3	Search the database for specific information	1
4	Create a spreadsheet	2
5	Amend the database table	1
6	Create a database report	1
7	Design a poster	1
8	Create a letter	1
9	Create an itinerary	1

- Always use your spellcheck
- Print each task
- Ensure you save all tasks as you complete them – you will need them again!

TASK 1

Create letter headed paper to be used by Elite Travel using the contact details below.

- use a variety of fonts/styles
- centre the information
- include a graphic of your choice

Elite Travel
140 George Street
Edinburgh
EH3 4JY

Telephone:
0131 248 5657
E-mail:
enquire@elite.co.uk

TASK 2

Customer details are currently held on record cards, but it has been decided to computerise all the records.

- Create a database called *Elite Travel* and a table called *Customers* containing the following fields and formatted as indicated:

FIELD NAME	FORMAT
Title	Text
First Name	Text
Surname	Text
Street	Text
Town	Text
Postcode	Text
Contact Tel No	Text
E-mail Address	Text
Booking Ref	Number
Deposit Paid	Yes/No
Amount of Deposit	Currency (0 decimal places)

- Create a form which includes all fields – use 'Customer Details' as the heading of the form. Use the form to input the data to the right and on p 71.

Title	Mr
First Name	John
Surname	Gilchrist
Street	54 Craigleith Drive
Town	Edinburgh
Postcode	EH12 6HE
Contact Tel No	01312931022
E-mail Address	
Booking Ref	4859
Deposit Paid	Yes
Amount of Deposit	£100

Title	MrS
First Name	Joan
Surname	Willis
Street	12 Marchmont Gardens
Town	Edinburgh
Postcode	EH14 7YE
Contact Tel No	01316364875
E-mail Address	
Booking Ref	5241
Deposit Paid	No
Amount of Deposit	

Title	Mr
First Name	Patrick
Surname	Green
Street	16 West Linton Road
Town	Edinburgh
Postcode	EH43 9LK
Contact Tel No	01316524153
E-mail Address	pgreen@vmail.co.uk
Booking Ref	4897
Deposit Paid	Yes
Amount of Deposit	£75

Title	Mr
First Name	Simon
Surname	Mann
Street	92 Cedar Way
Town	Haddington
Postcode	EH41 5TR
Contact Tel No	08877963852
E-mail Address	simon@quikmail.com
Booking Ref	4869
Deposit Paid	Yes
Amount of Deposit	£120

Title	Mr
First Name	Connor
Surname	O'Brien
Street	184 The Loaning
Town	Edinburgh
Postcode	EH18 9FG
Contact Tel No	01316548723
E-mail Address	
Booking Ref	4397
Deposit Paid	No
Amount of Deposit	

Title	Dr
First Name	George
Surname	Smith
Street	91 Pentland View
Town	Penicuik
Postcode	EH28 5RW
Contact Tel No	01312478493
E-mail Address	geosmith@bnet.com
Booking Ref	5132
Deposit Paid	Yes
Amount of Deposit	£125

Title	Mrs
First Name	Celia
Surname	Jackson
Street	63 Muir Road
Town	Currie
Postcode	EH14 6YH
Contact Tel No	08877321654
E-mail Address	cj@bnet.com
Booking Ref	5135
Deposit Paid	Yes
Amount of Deposit	£80

Title	Mrs
First Name	Aysha
Surname	Patel
Street	87 Green Road
Town	Penicuik
Postcode	EH21 7FD
Contact Tel No	01315857421
E-mail Address	
Booking Ref	5048
Deposit Paid	Yes
Amount of Deposit	£125

Title	Ms
First Name	Samantha
Surname	Arthur
Street	193 Afton Road
Town	Penicuik
Postcode	EH26 8LK
Contact Tel No	07788584269
E-mail Address	sarthur@bnet.com
Booking Ref	5167
Deposit Paid	Yes
Amount of Deposit	£85

Title	Mr
First Name	Andrew
Surname	Smith
Street	12 Winston Green
Town	Haddington
Postcode	EH41 5RE
Contact Tel No	01312588787
E-mail Address	
Booking Ref	5341
Deposit Paid	No
Amount of Deposit	

- Print the record for Mr Andrew Smith in form view
- Print the table sorted in descending order of Amount of Deposit on one page

 TASK 3

- Search the database you created in Task 2 to find those customers who have not paid a deposit. Include their Title, First Name and Surname in your search
- Print the results of this search

 TASK 4

Erin wants to know the total amount of all deposits that have been paid and the total amount outstanding that still has to be paid by customers who have made a booking. She also wants to know the minimum, the maximum and the average of these and the total number of customers.

- Create a spreadsheet with the following information
- Increase the font size of the main heading
- Embolden the main heading and the column headings
- Wrap text and format for currency (0 decimal places)
- Insert formulae where you see ?
- Sort the spreadsheet into ascending order of Balance Outstanding
- Print one copy of the completed spreadsheet showing figures and including gridlines
- Print one copy of the completed spreadsheet showing formulae, including row and column headings and gridlines

	A	B	C	
1	HOLIDAY BOOKINGS			
2	Booking Reference	Deposit Paid	Cost of Holiday	Balance Outstanding
3		4859	£100	£980	?
4		5241	£0	£335	?
5		4897	£75	£450	?
6		5132	£125	£1,200	?
7		5167	£85	£890	?
8		4869	£120	£1,150	?
9		5135	£80	£910	?
10		5341	£0	£325	?
11		4397	£0	£295	?
12		5048	£125	£1,350	?
13	TOTAL	?		?
14				
15	Average	?	?	?
16	Minimum	?	?	?
17	Maximum	?	?	?
18	Number of Customers	?		

IT SOLUTIONS FOR ADMINISTRATORS (CONTD)

⊙ TASK 5

Recall the database table: Customers

- Add a new field called Destination. Update the table with the following information *Hint: to make it easier to input the information sort the table by Surname first*
- Sort by destination then surname
- Print the results of your search on one page

Title	First Name	Surname	Destination
Ms	Samantha	Arthur	Madrid
Mr	John	Gilchrist	Stockholm
Mr	Patrick	Green	Prague
Mrs	Celia	Jackson	Stockholm
Mr	Simon	Mann	New York
Mr	Connor	O'Brien	Paris
Mrs	Aysha	Patel	New York
Dr	George	Smith	New York
Mr	Andrew	Smith	Prague
Mrs	Joan	Willis	Prague

⊙ TASK 6

- Search the database for customers who are going to New York. Also include the following fields: Title, First Name, Surname and Deposit Paid in your query.
- Print the results of your query in the form of a report using all fields except Destination. Use the title NEW YORK CUSTOMERS.

⊙ TASK 7

Erin would like to advertise the services of Elite Travel by placing posters in the local tourist information office and noticeboards in the local supermarkets. Using the details below, design a suitable poster.

- Make full use of an A4 sheet (either landscape or portrait)
- Include the graphic you used in TASK 1 and any other graphic you think relevant
- Use a variety of fonts and styles
- Insert a page border

Elite Travel

We offer:

A friendly service

Value-for-money holidays to suit all budgets and tastes

Package and tailor-made holidays available

Accommodation searches

Destinations include Edinburgh, London, Paris, Amsterdam and New York

Come in and see us now!

We are at 140 George Street, Edinburgh. Telephone us on: 0131 248 5657 or e-mail us at enquire@elite.co.uk

SPECIAL OFFER – 10% DISCOUNT ON ALL RESERVATIONS BOOKED THIS MONTH!

TASK 8

- Use the letter headed paper you created in TASK 1.
- Key in the following letter that will be signed by Erin. Use the standard layout of a business letter.
- The letter is going to Dr George Smith (booking ref 5132) – you will find his address in the database table – and look at the spreadsheet for the amount of deposit he has paid and the amount outstanding that he has still to pay.

Dear Dr Smith

OUTSTANDING BALANCE

It is now almost 6 weeks until your departure on holiday to New York. You have paid a deposit of (*see spreadsheet*) and the total cost of your holiday is (*see spreadsheet*). The difference is now due and should be paid to us as soon as possible. We can accept payment by credit or debit card – just phone us on the above number. We will send you a finalised itinerary once the full payment for your holiday has been received.

In the meantime, please get in touch if there is anything else we can do for you.

Bon voyage!

Yours sincerely

Erin Jones
Head of Reservations

TASK 9

Please draft up the itinerary which will be sent to Dr Smith one week prior to his departure.

ITINERARY: DR GEORGE SMITH

TRIP TO NEW YORK

1–6 February 20__

1 February

0730 hours   Flight AA876 departs Edinburgh airport for New York Newark airport – flight time 7 hours 35 minutes

1005 hours   Arrive New York Newark airport. NJ Taxis will meet you in the arrivals hall and take you to Central Park Hotel, 1289 5th Avenue, Manhattan

3 February

0930 hours   Meet our representative Steve in the hotel lobby and join our complimentary city tour – please quote tour reference ET6189. The tour will include lunch at the Brooklyn Diner

1530 hours   Return to hotel

5 February

1700 hours   NJ Taxis will pick you up from the hotel lobby and take you to New York Newark airport

1940 hours   Flight AA877 departs New York Newark airport for Edinburgh – flight time 6 hours 55 minutes

6 February

0635 hours   Flight arrives Edinburgh airport

ONLINE COMMUNICATION AND EMERGING TECHNOLOGIES

COMMUNICATING ONLINE AND TECHNOLOGICAL INNOVATIONS

Organisations operate within a dynamic and ever-changing environment and the use of emerging technologies, particularly computers and mobile devices, has impacted on the work and duties of the administrative assistant.

DEVELOPMENTS IN HARDWARE

Developments in **hardware** include 'smart' devices, for example, smartphones, which not only allow text and verbal communication but also face-to-face communication, web browsing and downloading, access to internal and external networks, e-mail capability, document creation and editing and access to social media. Computer programs or 'apps' can be downloaded, allowing the user to carry out a vast number of operations very easily.

DEVELOPMENTS IN SOFTWARE

There are also changes in the **software** that is being used. While the Microsoft Office suite of integrated software applications is still the most popular collection of titles used by administrators, organisations are looking for cost savings on IT expenditure and a growing number are now using alternative free integrated office suites such as OpenOffice, Google docs, LibreOffice and Zoho.

OTHER SIGNIFICANT DEVELOPMENTS

Social media

Other significant developments are the use of 'social media' such as Facebook, Twitter, LinkedIn, Google+, Pinterest, Skype, Facetime, Google Talk and Microsoft Messenger by organisations. These websites and applications encourage two-way and instant communication between employees, customers and suppliers and can be used to pass and receive information. Don't forget blogs and discussion groups which also allow people to post their thoughts and opinions which others can read and then respond to.

Online collaboration

Online collaboration has also become more accessible. Organisations can make use of web-based facilities that allow a number of users to access and contribute to the creation and development of documents, whether they are working from home or in the office. Online collaboration forums are beneficial for tasks that require team working and are suited to the development of creative ideas or complex documents, for example, those required for meetings and events. There is the opportunity for partnership working with customers and suppliers who can view and comment on live documents as they are being produced.

Presentation software

There have also been developments in presentation software. Microsoft PowerPoint, with an estimated 500 million users around the globe, is still the key presentation application used in the workplace. However, some would argue that it is overused and a number of organisations have sought alternatives that allow information to be presented in fresh and engaging ways. This has resulted in a number of web-based, non-linear presentation applications being developed. Instead of presenting information on a series of slides, users lay out information on a 'canvass' and then choose a path (the order) for presenting this information to their audience. Some organisations also make use of software that allows presentations to be saved as video files so that they can be uploaded later to intranets, websites and social media sites.

BENEFITS TO ADMINISTRATORS

Technology has also improved the personal effectiveness of administrators who are always looking to manage and use their time more efficiently. Administrators can prioritise and monitor the progress of tasks by making use of online To-Do lists as well as diary and reminder systems which can be accessed from a variety of devices including PCs and smartphones.

Cloud computing

Technological change has also had an impact on **Networks**. This is evident in Cloud computing which means storing and accessing data and programs over the internet instead of using the computer's hard drive. This saves organisations time and effort downloading, installing and keeping software up-to-date and it is more convenient for users as they are able to access cloud resources from any device that can be connected to the internet.

File conversion

Another useful tool available to administrators is the ability to convert a document or media file from one file type to another. For some conversions online sites are used, for example, a pdf file to Word.

Online tools

Online questionnaire and poll generation websites are also of great benefit to administrators. These sites make it easy to create surveys that can then be included on an organisation's website, social media site or intranet. Responses can be gathered and an administrative assistant can use the feedback to evaluate the success of an event.

Online video-hosting websites, such as YouTube, are also being widely used for a variety of purposes. For example, administrative assistants can watch video tutorials on the use of particular software to increase their skills, or they may be given the task of uploading a video onto the organisation's website or social media site.

USING THE INTERNET

As an administrative assistant you may be required to use the internet on an almost daily basis for a variety of purposes, for example, researching and booking travel and accommodation for your boss who is going on a business trip, finding out about the most current health and safety legislation, buying products from suppliers or dealing with customer queries.

Search engines

Using a search engine such as Google, Yahoo! or Bing can make the task of researching and finding information quick and easy. To carry out a search as efficiently as possible, try to think of a specific key word or phrase that best describes what you are looking for. Relevant information can then be downloaded onto your computer or you can select specific text on a web page and copy and paste into a Word document or presentation file. Remember to add appropriate acknowledgement to any copied text.

Bookmarking

Websites that you visit on a regular basis can be bookmarked or added to your Favourites to ensure quick and easy access and to avoid wasting time.

Staying safe

For the most part the internet is an invaluable tool, but always make sure you are using reliable websites that give up-to-date information. Anyone can create a website so always use those produced by reputable companies or organisations, for example, government websites. Make sure any personal or financial information is only uploaded onto sites that display a padlock at the bottom right-hand corner of the screen or contain https in the address. Accessing some sites may lead to viruses being downloaded that corrupt your hard drive, so it is important that anti-virus software is installed and you do not visit any sites where risks are highlighted.

Using unreliable sources of information can lead to serious consequences, for example, using an out-of-date travel timetable may mean that your boss is late for his meeting; if a secure website is not used then sensitive personal or financial information may be stolen; and not knowing the source of information might produce a report that is biased or contains inaccurate information. This could lead to poor decision-making which can be costly to the company or the organisation gaining a bad reputation.

THINGS TO DO AND THINK ABOUT

1. Not sure what apps are? Have a look at www.bbc.co.uk/webwise/guides/what-are-apps
2. Have a look at www.gcflearnfree.org/beyonde-mail to learn more about this topic and do the interactive quiz.
3. Have a look at www.gcflearnfree.org/internet101/5 for hints to improve your use of search engines.

DON'T FORGET

An *intra*net is a network that is only available to people within the same organisation. The *inter*net is available to every user all over the world.

PRESENTATION SOFTWARE – POWERPOINT

CREATING A PRESENTATION 1

INTRODUCTION

PowerPoint software allows you to create and show slides to support a presentation. By connecting your computer to a digital projector, slides can be displayed on a screen, providing a good way of giving information to a group of people. Text, graphics, charts, videos and sounds can be combined to make the presentation more interesting and engage the audience.

PowerPoint has become enormously popular and you are likely to have seen it being used by your teachers and fellow students or in presentations outside school. Learning to present with PowerPoint will increase your employability, as it is the world's most popular presentational software.

HOME

When creating a presentation you can use the **Home** tab to add **New Slides** and to decide what **Layout** you would like. There are nine basic layouts to choose from.

Slide Layouts are made up of **placeholders** (areas on the slide that are enclosed by dotted borders) and they can contain text, pictures and charts. Many are set up to automatically to give you bullet points. Some have **thumbnail-sized icons** that represent specific commands such as Insert Picture or Insert ClipArt.

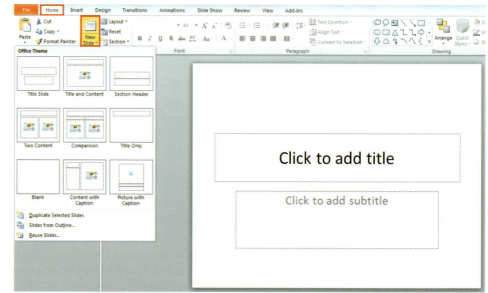

DON'T FORGET

When you open a blank presentation in PowerPoint, the default layout **Title Slide** appears – you can change this by clicking on Layout and selecting the one you want.

Placeholders can be deleted from the slide if they are not required.

DON'T FORGET

You can also insert text by drawing Text Boxes.

DESIGN

The **Design** tab lets you choose the design or **theme** of your slides.

A **theme** is a set of colours, fonts and effects that can be applied to the entire presentation to give it a consistent, professional look without having to spend a lot of time formatting each slide. Once you have selected a theme you can make further changes to the colours, fonts, etc. to suit your purpose. Themes can be applied or changed at any time as you work through your presentation.

Using the down arrow at the right-hand side will give you more options – there are many themes to choose from.

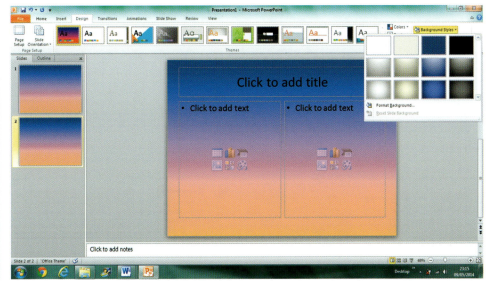

If you want to keep the theme of your slide simpler then **Background Styles**, with shading and colour options, are available.

DON'T FORGET

It is often easier to apply a theme *before* you start building your presentation as you will be able to arrange your content to fit the layouts available within that theme. If you apply the theme *after* you start building, then the text boxes and placeholders within the slides may move depending upon the theme you have chosen.

TRANSITIONS

Transitions are motion effects that add movement to slides as one slide advances to the next in Slide Show View. There are many transitions to choose from and you can even control the speed, add sound or have the slides advance automatically – this means the presenter does not have to click on the mouse or press the enter key!

Again the list can be expanded to show more options. If you want to have the same transition for every slide click on Apply To All.

THINGS TO DO AND THINK ABOUT

The Preview button at the top left-hand side of the ribbon will show you the effect you have chosen. Try this for yourself – open a new PowerPoint presentation and apply a transition effect of your choice to the opening slide. Have a look at all the options.

DON'T FORGET

To remove transitions from **all slides**, select a slide that uses **None**, and click the Apply to All command at the right on the ribbon.

CREATING A PRESENTATION 2

ANIMATIONS

In PowerPoint you can add movement to text, clip art objects, shapes and pictures to draw the audience's attention to specific content or to make the slide easier to read. You can even use **motion paths** to create a customised animation.

DON'T FORGET

Well-placed animations can help emphasise important points or information – too many animations can become distracting for your audience!

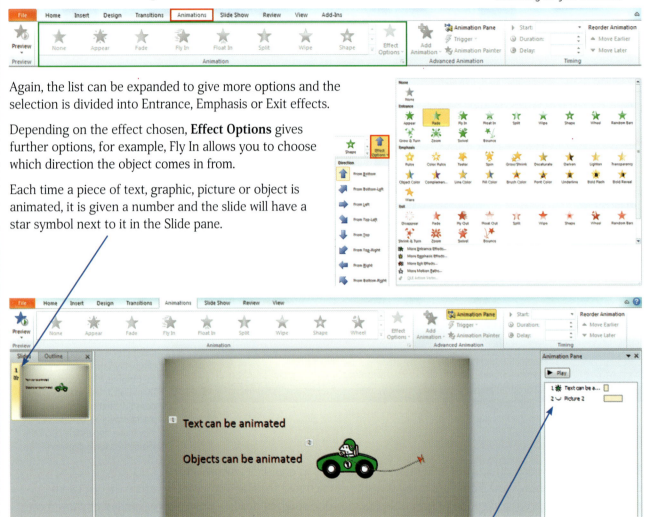

Again, the list can be expanded to give more options and the selection is divided into Entrance, Emphasis or Exit effects.

Depending on the effect chosen, **Effect Options** gives further options, for example, Fly In allows you to choose which direction the object comes in from.

Each time a piece of text, graphic, picture or object is animated, it is given a number and the slide will have a star symbol next to it in the Slide pane.

These numbers help edit animation effects and, using the **Animation Pane**, changes can be made to the effects.

EXAMPLE

To add multiple animations to an object:

When a new animation is added to an object it will **replace** the object's current animation. To place **more than one animation** on an object, for example, an **Entrance** and an **Exit** effect, use the **Add Animation** command. This will allow the current animation and a new one. If the object has more than one effect, it will have a different number for each effect. The numbers indicate the **order** in which the effects will occur.

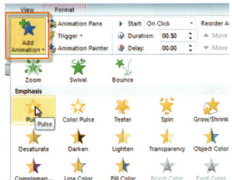

VIEW

Slide Master view

Slide Master view allows you to modify slides and slide layouts in your presentation which will affect **EVERY** slide in the presentation, for example, insert the company logo on all slides. This can save a lot of time. **Themes** have built-in slide layouts and background graphics and these can be edited in **Slide Master** view. It is also possible to modify individual slide layouts which will change any slides using those layouts.

Hover the mouse over the remaining layouts to see which slides use which particular layouts. Changes to a slide layout will **only** be applied to slides using that layout in your presentation – in this case only slides 2–4 and no other.

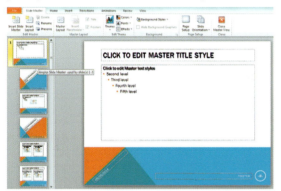
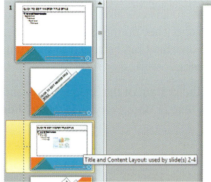

After you have made changes to the **Slide Master,** it is a good idea to review your presentation to see how it affects each slide. You may find that some of your slides don't look exactly right and more changes will have to be made! Close Master View to return to your presentation.

Slide Sorter

This allows changes to be made to the order slides are shown – it is simply a case of clicking on the slide you want to move and dragging it into the new position.

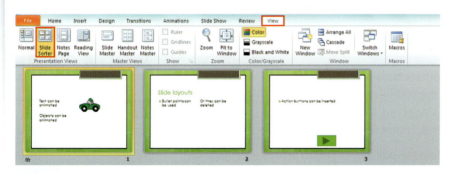

THINGS TO DO AND THINK ABOUT

Try this for yourself with any presentation you have already created and saved – move the last slide to become the first slide and the first slide to become the last one.

DON'T FORGET

When editing an **existing** presentation it is sometimes easier to see which layouts have been used if you first delete those layouts 'used by no slides'.

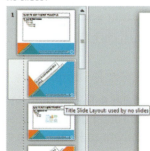

CREATING A PRESENTATION 3

INSERT

The **Insert** tab is similar to that used in Word – from here you can insert Pictures, Clip Art, Text Boxes, Word Art, Shapes, and so on.

Action Buttons

Within **Shapes** you can select **Action Buttons** – Action Button shapes can be added to a presentation and set to link one slide to another when someone clicks on or moves over the shape. They do the same job as hyperlinks and, because they are easy to use, they can be added to self-running presentations at booths or kiosks.

Actions buttons are found at the bottom of the Shapes menu and can either be inserted into one slide at a time or onto every slide using **Slide Master**.

EXAMPLE

To insert Action Buttons:

Select the button you want, for example, the forward button to take you to the next slide, then draw the shape on your slide.

When the shape has been drawn in the desired position, the **Action Settings** dialogue box opens. Check which slide the link is being made to and then click OK.

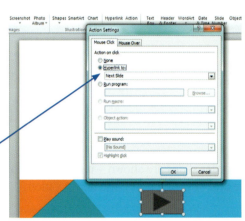

Header & Footer/Slide Number

Header & Footer and **Slide Number** buttons both open the **Header and Footer** dialogue box and give you the option of inserting slide numbers and a footer on all slides (click Apply to All) or only on the slide you are in when you select Header & Footer (click Apply).

The **Notes and Handouts** tab in this dialogue box allows you to set up headers and footers and page numbers, should you choose to print in handout format rather than each whole slide.

DON'T FORGET

The position of the slide number and headers/footers can vary depending on the Theme that has been chosen.

SLIDE SHOW

This allows the slide show to be run on the full size of the screen. You can start from the beginning of the show or from the current slide.

PRINTING YOUR PRESENTATION

Print is accessed from the **File** tab. Using the down arrow beside **Full Page Slides** you can see the options that are available for printing your presentation, for example, 1 slide per page **or** 3 slides plus space for notes **or** 6 or 9 slides per page.

Headers and Footers can also be edited directly from this screen.

THINGS TO DO AND THINK ABOUT

Once you are happy with the information on the last four pages, head to www.brightredbooks.net/N5AdminIT for some great practical tasks on presentation software.

DESKTOP PUBLISHING

USING DESKTOP PUBLISHING SOFTWARE

INTRODUCTION

While posters, notices, booklets and brochures can all be produced using a word processing package such as Word, there is also the option of using desktop publishing (DTP) software such as Publisher which contains a lot of templates (either installed or available online), wizards and layouts to make the job easier.

USING A TEMPLATE

Templates come with text and graphics in placeholders. These can be edited, rearranged by dragging them around the page or deleted to reflect the way you want your layout to look and your own boxes can be added. Once you have chosen a template, there are further options to choose colour schemes and font schemes using the pane on the right.

EXAMPLE

Here is an example of some of the Menu templates that are available:

CREATING YOUR OWN PUBLICATION

As an alternative to using a template you can create your own design. Just remember, Publisher 'works' by putting every element into a box – text, graphics, logos and pictures go into their own box and each box is layered onto the page. It is a good idea before starting your publication that you plan how you want it to look – decide on size, orientation, use of columns and placement of graphics relative to text.

Booklets

Booklets are very easy to produce. Some booklet layouts to be considered using A4 landscape include:

Half Fold   **Tri-Fold**   **Z-Fold**   **Accordian**

EXAMPLE

To create a tri-fold booklet:

Start with a New Blank A4 (Landscape) page:

Now go to the Page Design tab and under Margins select Custom Margins

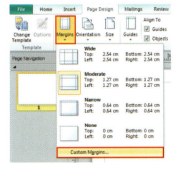 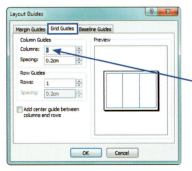

When the Layout Guides dialogue box appears, select the Grid Guides tab then select either 3 or 4 columns depending on how you want to fold your finished booklet.

This will give you one side of your booklet.

When you want to add another side simply right-click on the first page in the Page Navigation pane and select Insert Duplicate Page.

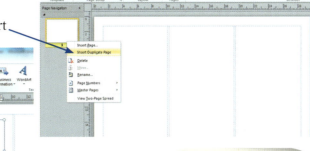

Now you have both sides and you can start your booklet.

To add text go to the Insert tab then Draw Text Box. Start keying in your text. Additional Text Box Tools and Drawing Tools will become available which will give more formatting and layout options.

PRINTING

It is more than likely that you will want to print on both sides of your page. Check that your printer will allow this and choose this option from the Print menu.

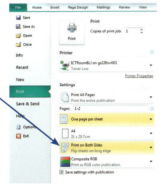

DON'T FORGET

In order to see your page more clearly you will have to zoom in using the bar at the bottom right of your screen.

DON'T FORGET

Remember to place text, graphics and logos in their own 'box' when adding them to your publication.

THINGS TO DO AND THINK ABOUT

Now try this task which will test your knowledge of DTP software as well as your skills in changing fonts, line spacing, text formatting and layout.

ONLINE

Head to www.brightredbooks.net/N5AdminIT for an extra task.

TASK

1. Create the tri-fold leaflet shown. Start by setting up your document as A4 landscape with three columns and then create a duplicate second page.

2. Search the internet for suitable graphics and ensure you use a variety of fonts and formats. Print double-sided when completed, with your name in the footer.

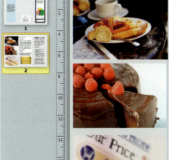

BUSINESS CARDS, NAME BADGES AND EVENT TICKETS

AN OVERVIEW

These types of publications usually measure about 8.5 cm by 5.5 cm. This means that the card or ticket can be designed then repeated across and down an A4 sheet and then guillotined or cut.

Business cards

Business cards contain information about a company or individual. They are usually passed from one person to another during introductions as a memory aid. A business card typically includes the person's name, job title, company or business name (usually with a logo) and contact information such as postal address, telephone numbers (landline and mobile), e-mail address, website and Facebook and Twitter usernames.

Name badges

Name badges are worn so that individuals can be identified by others. They contain relevant information about the person – their name, job title and perhaps a graphic.

Event tickets

Event tickets will contain information such as the name, date, time, place and price of the event along with some graphics.

Templates for these types of documents are available, but it is possible to design your own.

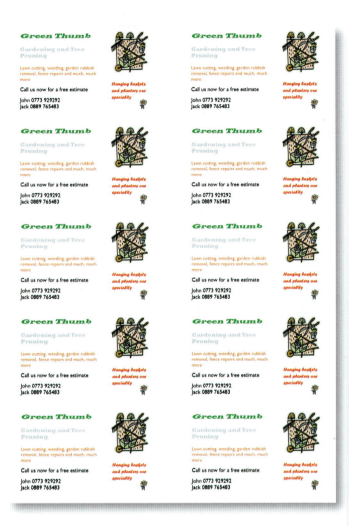

EXAMPLE

To create a business card

Select Business Cards from the Available Templates.

Scroll down in the next window and, under Blank Sizes, select European Size in landscape orientation.

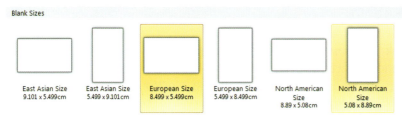

Then click create:  . This provides you with a blank canvass to create the business card that you want. The card will automatically be copied on the page when it is printed.

+ DON'T FORGET

Business cards help to sell the business – make sure all contact details are included as well as a brief summary of the services provided.

THINGS TO DO AND THINK ABOUT

TASK 1

1. Set up a blank business card and create one similar to that shown opposite using different fonts, formats and relevant graphics found on the internet.
2. When complete proof-read carefully and print 10 business cards per page – the computer will automatically size your business cards to allow this.

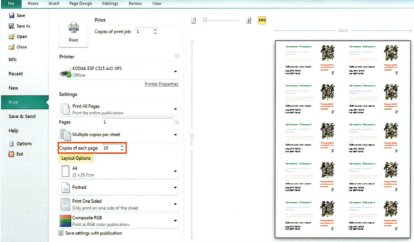

TASK 2

1. Create a business card for Jason Clark, owner of Windowbrite. His business is window and conservatory cleaning. His address is 30 Dummer Drive, Glasgow, G13 7PR. His mobile telephone number is 07382 221788. He can be contacted evenings and weekends on 0141 6602456. His e-mail address is jclark@btnet.com and he has a page on Facebook.
2. Include relevant graphics and use a variety of fonts and styles.
3. Proof-read the business card then print 10 copies per page.

COMMUNICATIONS SOFTWARE

USING OUTLOOK

Communications software, such as Outlook, lets you send, receive and manage e-mails and also manage your calendar and contacts, such as friends and business associates. In addition, Outlook offers a task management facility as well as electronic "sticky notes".

OPENING OUTLOOK

When Outlook opens you will get a window similar to that shown below. Under the Home tab you can either click on **New E-mail** to compose a new message or on **New Items** where, as well as being able to select E-mail Message, you will also be able to set up a new **Appointment**, **Contact** or **Task**. Going further down the menu to More Items, you will also be able to access **Note** – these are like sticky notes where you can add brief messages to yourself.

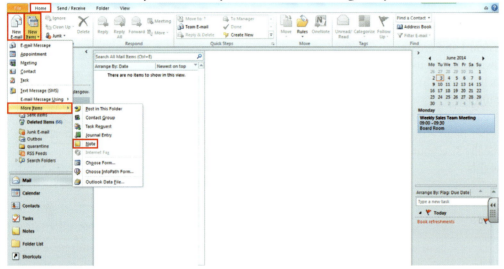

You can also access these functions by clicking on the icons in the navigation pane. We will now look at each of these individually.

MAIL

Electronic mail, or e-mail, is like sending a letter only the letter is sent over the intranet or internet and the recipient receives the message within seconds rather than days. E-mails can be received on smartphones and laptops as well as desktops. In order to save time, e-mail addresses can be saved in **Contacts** and **Contact Groups** (otherwise known as distribution lists) which can be set up to include groups of people that you might e-mail on a regular basis. For example, Mr Jones, a teacher, might set up a contact group consisting of the e-mail addresses of all pupils in his Admin class.

Sending a message

Clicking on New E-mail will open a window which will allow you to compose a new message. You can either key in the e-mail address of the recipient or if you click on To... this will take you into your list of contacts and allow you to select the appropriate address. A number of e-mail addresses can be put in the address box. Entering an e-mail address in the Cc... box will mean that the recipient will also receive a copy of the message – this is normally just to keep them informed of what is happening; they do not need to take any action.

To send a document or file with your message use **Attach File** and if the e-mail is urgent mark it with **High Importance**.

E-MAIL GUIDELINES

The following guidelines suggest how an e-mail should be composed:

- Include a Subject – what the e-mail is about.
- Start the e-mail with the person's name, 'Good Morning/Afternoon' or, when sending to a group, you could use something along the lines of 'Colleagues'.
- Keep the message brief and to the point. Do not use ALL CAPS – this means that you are shouting! Check all spelling and grammar carefully. Does the message make sense?
- Make it clear in the message if there is an attachment.
- Let the reader know that you have finished your message by including a closing line of text or 'Regards' or 'Best wishes' or something similar.
- Use attachments to send files, pictures or large documents. However, be careful with attachments you receive as this is one of the most common ways for computer viruses to spread. As a rule, you should never open an attachment from someone you don't know or trust. Even if you know the sender, don't open an attachment you are not expecting or an attachment that looks suspicious. Some viruses can destroy all the data on your computer, so it's best to play it safe!
- If a message is very important it can be marked with a symbol which indicates that it should be read as a priority. Click on ❗ **High Importance**.

DON'T FORGET

Take time to clean out your inbox on a regular basis – any e-mails you want to keep can be organised into folders.

REPLYING TO A MESSAGE

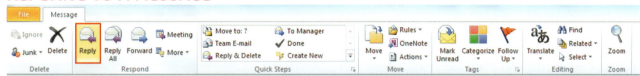

To reply to a message that has been received, click on Reply. A window will open showing the original message as well as providing space for your reply.

PRINTING E-MAILS

Any e-mail that has been sent or received can be printed. Simply select the e-mail, go to the File tab then Print in Memo Style. Printing an e-mail will show details of date and time that the e-mail was actually sent as well as the message.

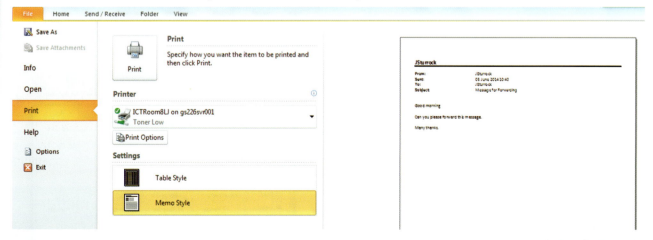

 THINGS TO DO AND THINK ABOUT

Once you are happy with the information about communications software in this section, try out the practical exercises on pages 89 and 91.

ONLINE

For some great practical tasks on communications software, head to www.brightredbooks.net/N5AdminIT

CALENDAR

The e-diary facility within Outlook is a way of keeping a record of appointments and meetings on computer. Features of an e-diary include:

- Diaries can be viewed by day, week or month.

- Reminders can be set.

- Access levels can be set so that only each individual can view and enter their appointments or so that the diaries of several people can be linked and appointments that suit all can be found.

- Invitations to meetings can be sent and recipients can either accept or decline the invitation – if they accept, their diary will be updated to reflect this new appointment.

- Double bookings will be highlighted as will any overlapping appointments.

- An appointment that occurs at the same time every day, week or month need only be entered once and the appointment will be automatically entered for that time and day until a stop date is entered. Such appointments are known as recurring appointments.

- Records of past diary appointments can be kept for a very long time and diaries are able to record appointments many years into the future!

USING THE CALENDAR

Clicking on **Calendar** in the navigation pane will open your diary in a view that will include today's date – you can view your diary in a variety of Arrangements.

To create a new entry for your diary click on New Appointment in the Home tab and the following window will open:

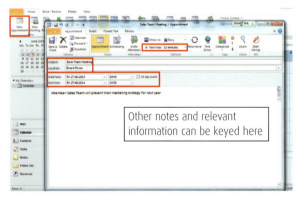

Other notes and relevant information can be keyed here

DON'T FORGET ✚

Double click on any saved appointments to make any amendments.

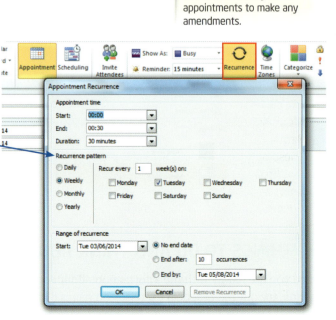

Details of the appointment can be added in the **Subject** box and the venue can be put in the **Location** box. **Start time** and **End time** or **All day event** can be selected. To ensure that the appointment is not forgotten, a **Reminder** can be set.

Finally, if the meeting occurs on the same day and at the same time on a regular basis, the appointment can be automatically entered into the diary for the coming weeks and months by clicking on **Recurrence** and setting up as appropriate.

Remember to click on OK then Save & Close to save the appointment.

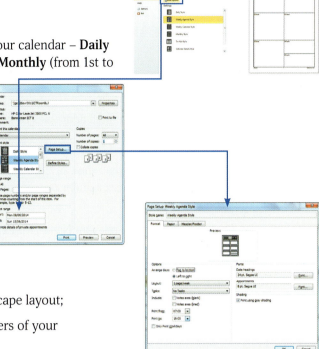

PRINTING YOUR DIARY

There are a number of options available when printing your calendar – **Daily Style** (print only one day), **Weekly** (Monday–Sunday) or **Monthly** (from 1st to the last day of the month).

Print Options

Clicking on **Print Options** will allow you to print only the dates you want and not the whole year.

Page Setup

From **Page Setup**, in the Print dialogue box you can make further changes to the layout of your print:

Format tab will allow you to change the times within the days that are printed, especially if there are evening appointments;

Paper tab will allow you to change from portrait to landscape layout;

Header/Footer tab will allow changes to headers and footers of your printed diary.

THINGS TO DO AND THINK ABOUT

Now try some of these exercises which will test your knowledge of electronic diary software.

TASK 1

Interviews for the post of Senior Administrative Assistant are being held next Friday and you have to record candidates' names and appointment times in your electronic diary.

- Mr Jordan Smith is being interviewed at 9.30 am, followed by Mr Walter Darcy at 10.30 am and finally Mrs Frances Hogan at 11.30 am. All interviews are being held in the Board Room. Allow 45 minutes for each appointment.
- A reminder should be set 15 minutes prior to each appointment.
- Print an extract from the diary in daily view.

TASK 2

The first full week of next month is going to be very busy in the office and there are a number of appointments that need to be added to the diary. Please enter the following and print an extract for the week showing all appointments:

- Monday 10.00–11.00 am Sales Team review meeting to be held in Conference Room 1.
- Tuesday 12.30 pm lunch with Mr Stephen Jones, Bank Manager, at the Royal Hotel, Smithton. This is likely to last until 2.00 pm.
- Thursday 3.00 pm – meeting with Ms Penny Forrest and Mr Graham Whyte, Advertising Scotland plc, at their offices at 202 George Street, Glasgow. This meeting will last for 2 hours.
- Friday morning has been set aside for staff appraisal meetings – these normally last for one hour. The first meeting will be with Gordon Black at 9.30 am, then Jenny Jones at 10.30 and finally George Smith at 11.30 am. All these meetings will be held in Meeting Room 3.

DON'T FORGET

Diaries use a 24-hour clock format – you will have to convert the times given

DON'T FORGET

Your diary may be linked to your e-mail settings so check and see if your name is automatically included in the footer.

CONTACTS AND TASKS

CONTACTS

The e-mail address of anyone you e-mail on a regular basis can be added to your Contacts. This saves you having to remember e-mail addresses or key them in every time.

Contact group

If there is a set of people you regularly e-mail as a group, then you can create a **Contact Group** which will keep all their addresses under one name. When a message is sent, everyone in the group will receive it.

Start by giving the group of people a relevant Name, for example, N4/5 Admin & IT Students, then click on Members and add the contact details of each pupil to the group. This means that, instead of having to find 20 or so names individually each time you want to send the class an e-mail, you can go directly to that named Contact Group.

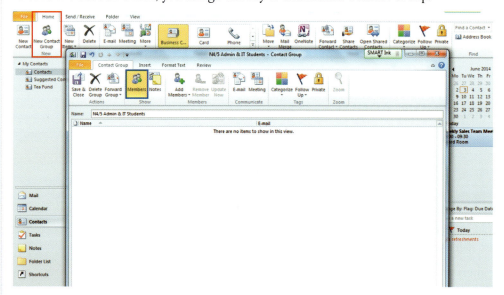

![PRACTICAL EXERCISE:]

Try it for yourself – set up a **Contact Group** made up of everyone in your class and send everyone a message.

TASKS

So that you won't forget to do important jobs, you can use the **Tasks** window in Outlook to list what you need to do and when you need to do it. You can allocate dates by which tasks have to be completed and prioritise according to urgency. The status of tasks can be updated according to progress – a grey line appears across tasks that you have completed; tasks that are overdue appear in red.

Tasks to be done can be entered by clicking on New Task in the Home tab.

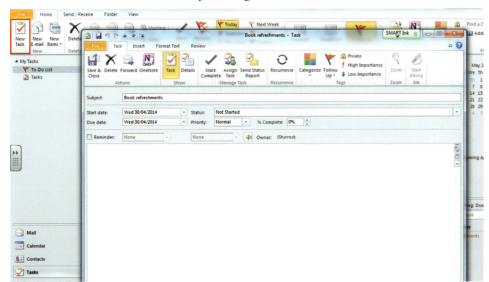

+ DON'T FORGET

Whenever you are asked to print a copy of your calendar and your tasks, use Print Preview to check that all the information can be read and none has been truncated (cut off). You might need to switch from portrait orientation to landscape.

THINGS TO DO AND THINK ABOUT

Now try some of these exercises which will test your knowledge of communications software.

TASK 1

There is going to be a Training Conference on the last Friday of next month (31 October). Enter the event as an all-day appointment. There are a number of important arrangements still to be finalised before the meeting, so add them to your Task list so that you don't forget – make the start date today and the end date the day before the conference.

- The digital projector is required for the whole day – check it is operational.
- Order 10 large bottles of water and glasses to be placed at the front of the room.
- Order tea/coffee and biscuits for 50 to be served at 10.30 am.
- Finalise lunch by next Thursday and ensure it will be served at 12.30 pm.

Print one copy of the Task list.

TASK 2

Enter the following appointments and tasks in your diary for the first week of May:

- Monday 9.00 am – Monthly Team Briefing which will last for one hour. From May this meeting will take place on the first Monday of every month, so make sure this is entered as a recurring meeting.
- Tuesday 10.30 am – Meeting with Mr Henry McLean, Area Sales Rep, Acme plc to discuss renewing supplies contract. Set a reminder 15 minutes before this meeting is due to begin.
- Wednesday 3.00 pm – Appraisal meeting with Chris King. This meeting will last 45 minutes.
- Friday 5.00 pm – Retiral Reception for Mr Sam Gray – this will be held in The Buttery. Add reminders to the task list to check first that drinks and canapes for 60 people have been ordered and second that the photographer has been booked.
- Print an extract of the diary for this week showing these appointments and the task list.

PRACTICE ASSIGNMENT

COMMUNICATION IN ADMINISTRATION

Mr Hugh Young, Head of the Modern Languages Department at Blairhill High School, has organised a 5-day trip to Paris next April to allow students to explore the capital city of France and also have the chance to try out their linguistic skills! Mr Young knows you are studying Administration and IT and has asked for your assistance in researching information and putting together some documents and files in preparation for the trip.

Set up a folder in your My Documents called **PARIS TRIP**. Save all tasks into this folder.

TASK 1

Set up an electronic To-Do list detailing the tasks that you have to complete:

1. Create an information sheet and e-mail it to Mr Young for his comments.
2. Research information about Parc Astérix and exchange rates.
3. Prepare a PowerPoint presentation for the meeting with parents.
4. Design name badges.

Print one copy of your task list.

TASK 2

All pupils are to take £100 spending money. Find out the current rate of exchange and how many Euros they will get for their £100. Print one copy of the internet page(s) giving you this information, as you will need it for Task 3 and Task 7. The rate of exchange changes on a daily basis and you might need to revisit the page(s) again immediately before the trip, so either bookmark it or add it to your favourites.

TASK 3

An information sheet outlining details of the trip is required. Key in the following text, add a page border, insert two or three appropriate graphics and make use of different font sizes and formats for the headings. Save the document as **PARIS INFO SHEET** and print one copy with your name in the footer.

MODERN LANGUAGES TRIP TO PARIS

INFORMATION SHEET

Our trip to the capital city of France will give pupils a taste of French culture, history, cuisine and language. This is our suggested itinerary:

Day	Activity
Friday	Travel to Château Grande, Antony Evening: Welcome tour & challenge
Saturday	Morning: Eiffel Tower and River Seine Cruise (Bateaux Parisiens) Afternoon: Notre Dame Cathedral Evening: Mini Olympics
Sunday	Morning: Chateau de Fontainebleau Afternoon: Visit to Snail Farm Evening: Choice of Recreation Activities
Monday	Full day at Parc Astérix Evening: Farewell party
Tuesday	Depart Paris to travel home

Places of interest

Eiffel Tower
Built in 1889, this ultimate symbol of Paris is the city's most-visited attraction and offers spectacular views from three levels.

Bateaux Parisiens
Departing from near the Eiffel Tower, this popular river sightseeing tour provides an opportunity to see and learn more about the main historical sites in the city.

Notre-Dame Cathedral
The historical cathedral of Notre-Dame is situated on Ile de la Cité. Climb the 387 steps to get a superb view of Paris and see the bell rung by Quasimodo!

Château de Fontainebleau
This impressive former royal residence dates back eight centuries. You will visit the state rooms and apartments of some of the famous people who lived there, including Marie Antoinette and Napoleon.

Snail Farm
The snail farm offers a good insight to rural French life. The owner will give a guided tour of the farm, in French, telling you everything that you need to know about snails and how the farm works.

Parc Astérix
A theme park with a very French feel. Share the adventures with Astérix and Obelix, including a huge variety of rides and the fantastic aquatic theatre.

The price of all these excursions has already been included in the cost of the trip and all you will need is spending money – we recommend you take no more than £100 which will give you €(**insert the number of Euros you found in Task 1 here**).

Here is a link to a map of Paris showing the locations of these famous landmarks (**search for a map of Paris showing sites and attractions and insert the web address as a hyperlink – check to ensure your link works**).

 TASK 4

Send an e-mail to Mr Young (use your teacher's e-mail address) and attach a copy of the information sheet you completed in Task 3. Ensure that Mr Young knows the e-mail contains an attachment and ask him if he would like any changes made to the document. Mark the e-mail as urgent. Print one copy of your sent e-mail.

COMMUNICATION IN ADMINISTRATION (CONTD)

TASK 5

In the run up to the trip Mr Young has to hold a number of meetings with parents, pupils and the headteacher, and he would like you to attend. Enter these in your electronic diary for next week and set 15 minute reminders for each appointment.

Monday 8.45–9.15 am. Meeting with Miss Jones, Headteacher in the Conference Room.

Wednesday 6.30 pm. Meeting with parents in the Assembly Hall. This meeting is scheduled to last one hour.

Friday 1.15–1.40 pm. Pupil meeting in the Assembly Hall.

Print an extract from your diary showing these appointments in weekly view.

TASK 6

Use the internet to find the website for Parc Astérix. Identify two rides that might appeal to the pupils going on the trip and copy and paste information about these rides into a Word document. Insert a title at the top and in the centre 'Parc Astérix'. Save the document as **PARC RIDES** and print one copy with your name in the footer.

TASK 7

Mr Young would like you to prepare a presentation that he can use at the parents' meeting. Using presentation software create the following slides. Choose a suitable background, insert an appropriate graphic on the first slide and animate all text. Apply a slide transition to all slides. Print the presentation in handout format with nine slides per page. Insert your name in the footer of the handout. Save the presentation as **PARIS ACCOMMODATION**.

Slide 1 – Title Slide layout

TRIP TO PARIS

Slide 2 – Title and Content layout

WHERE WE ARE STAYING

We are staying at Château Grande, Antony

This is a 19th Century château
set in 45 acres of land,
just 10 miles from Paris

Slide 3 – Title and Content layout

OUR ACCOMMODATION

Pupils will share six-bedded rooms
with single and bunk beds and
en suite facilities

Slide 4 – Title and Content layout

FACILITIES AT THE CHATEAU
Boules pitch
Full-size football pitch
Games room
Cinema room
Outdoor heated swimming pool
Tennis courts
(Make the above list bullet points)

Slide 5 – Title and Content layout with a table

ACTIVITIES AVAILABLE

Activity	Cost
Abseiling	£5
Archery	£3
Trapeze	£4
Zip Wire	£4

Swap the order of slides 5 and 6

Slide 6 – Title and Content layout

RECREATION ADVENTURE ACTIVITIES

Adventure activity sessions are
available at the Château for a
small supplement

Slide 7 – Title and Content layout

BOOKING ACTVITIES

- Pupils sign up for activities when they arrive
- Payment should be made in local currency
- £1 = ? **(insert a hyperlink here taking you to the exchange website you found in Task 1)**

Slide 8 – Title and Content layout

OUR ITINERARY

**(Insert a copy of the table outlining
the itinerary from the information
sheet you created in Task 3)**

Slide 9 – Title Only layout – move the Placeholder to the centre of the slide

Any other questions?

🎯 TASK 8

In order to identify all pupils belonging to our group, name badges will be issued. Using Publisher design a suitable badge – use a variety of fonts and shading, a suitable graphic and a border. At the moment just put in your name – you can edit the badges later once you have a final list of pupils going on the trip. Make sure you include the name of the school, Trip to Paris and the month and year of the trip. Save the document as **NAME BADGE** and print one sheet of name badges.

GLOSSARY

address labels
used to send out several letters at the same time. Address labels are created by merging the information on a database of addresses into a word document and then printing this onto labels.

agenda
is attached to the notice of meeting and provides an outline of what will be discussed at the meeting.

anti-virus software
software that detects viruses, data loggers and other electronic dangers

blog
an online journal commonly used to record a person's thoughts and feelings on a particular topic or theme

budget
an estimate of income and expenditure for a set period of time (used in the context of events in this guide)

business letter
a formal communication between an organisation and another interested party – for example, customers, shareholders, suppliers and employees. The template used for a business letter is called a letterhead.

cell reference
sometimes referred to as a cell address, a cell reference consists of the column letter and row number where the cell is located

charting
the graphic representation of numerical data. Charts can be used to present data in a format that is easy to read and interpret, and can also be used to highlight trends in the data. Spreadsheets enable you to create a variety of charts from their data.

comprehensive
including or dealing with all or nearly all elements or aspects of something

consequence
a result or effect of something

curriculum vitae (CV)
a document prepared by an individual who is looking for employment. This document will detail the person's skills, qualities, experience and qualifications.

customer service
the process of ensuring that the customer feels that the product or service they have bought has met or exceeded their expectations. Customer service is the process of ensuring that the customer feels that the product or service they have bought has met or exceeded their expectations.

Data Protection Act 1998
This Act states that organisations which hold personal data must ensure that the data is:
- held fairly and lawfully
- only used for the purpose registered with the Information Commissioner

- adequate, relevant and not excessive
- accurate
- not held for longer than is necessary
- held securely
- processed in line with the data subjects rights
- not transferred outside the EEA (European Economic Area).

database
software designed to store large amounts of data electronically so that it can be accessed by different users and presented in different ways

datasheet view
the view in database software that enables you to see all the records

design view
the view in database software that enables you to see the Field Names and Data Types

desktop publishing (DTP)
software used to place and manipulate text and graphics on your computer to produce print-ready, high-quality materials.

e-diary
an electronic scheduling tool that is normally linked to your e-mail account. It helps you to keep track of important dates, times of meetings and tasks with deadlines. Everyone in a team can share their e-diaries.

e-mail
The Oxford Online Dictionary defines e-mail as: 'Messages distributed by electronic means from one computer user to one or more recipients via a network.'

encryption
used to transfer sensitive data across the internet

event
in the context of Administration and IT, an event is a planned assembly of people, brought together for a related purpose or cause.

favourites and bookmarks
are browser functions that allow you to save a link to a web page that you access regularly, or would like to access again in the future.

form
a document that is designed to collect information from another person or group of people. It can be designed to be completed by hand or electronically. There are many different forms used in business:
- Application form
- Accident Report form
- Travel and accommodation booking form
- Expenses claim form.

function
a pre-set formula in spreadsheet software. Functions include:
- SUM
- AVERAGE
- MAX
- MIN
- COUNT (NUMBERS)

house style
a standard layout that an organisation uses in all of its documentation to ensure that everything it sends out to customers looks consistent, professional and instantly recognisable.

hyperlinks
used to move quickly between different pages on a website or around the internet in general.

IF statements
help to test a condition that is specified in a spreadsheet to see if it's true or false. If the condition is true, the function will carry out one action. If the condition is false, it will carry out a different action. You can then make a decision based on this information.

itinerary
a travel document that details the journey the person is taking, step by step.

job description
outlines the background to the role, the tasks/duties to be carried out, the employee's responsibilities and who they report to. It might also include their days/hours of work, pay grade and benefits.

line spacing
is the amount of space between each line. You can select the amount of line spacing you require – for example:
- 1 (single space)
- 1.5 (one-and-a-half space)
- 2 (double space).

manuscript corrections
a standard set of correction marks to show what editing is required (see p55).

memorandum
a word-processed document that is used to communicate information internally between different departments or between management and staff.

minutes of meeting
a written account of what was discussed at a meeting.

name badges
created in a similar way to address labels for people attending a conference or training event, for example.

notice of a meeting
sent out to those attending a meeting to inform them of the purpose of the meeting and when and where it will be held.

person specification
details the skills, qualities, qualifications and experience that a suitable candidate is required to have.

primary key
a field in a spreadsheet containing information that is unique to the record it is attached to. Examples include Customer Reference Numbers, National Insurance Numbers and SQA Numbers.

quality
a personal characteristic – something which describes the type of person you are.

repetitive strain injury
a term used to describe pain in the muscles, tendons and nerves. It is often caused by tasks of a repetitive nature such as using a keyboard, by poor posture or by incorrect positioning of seating.

retain
to keep hold of something.

search engine
helps you to find what you need by searching all the web pages available against criteria you have entered, and by filtering the results for you.

skill
an ability that is gained through learning and training.

slide transition
the process of moving between two slides in a presentation. Different types of slide transition can give your presentation a more controlled feel, and can also improve the experience for the viewer.

social media
essentially designed to allow people to share their lives with friends, family and business colleagues online – and to make new friends or contacts. Some examples of these are Facebook, Twitter, Instagram and Linkedin.

spreadsheet
an electronic document in which data is arranged in the rows and columns of a grid and can be manipulated and used in calculations. This software allows the user to perform complex calculations through the use of formulae and functions. Spreadsheets can be used to prepare financial statements and budgets. You can also use spreadsheet software to create visual aids such as charts and graphs.

template
a document that has been prepared in advance, and that often contains key information about a business.

text alignment
how text is lined up. Text is normally aligned to the left but you can highlight blocks of text and highlight them to the right, centre or on both sides.

to-do lists
a list of the tasks that have to be completed in a project.

venue
place where an organised event is held.

website
a dedicated site on a specific topic or theme. Websites have specific addresses on the internet called URLs – uniform resource locators.

workbook
a spreadsheet file.

worksheet
a single page within a spreadsheet file.